Rising Strong

A Survivor's Guide to Thriving After Domestic Violence

M L Rusenak

RISING STRONG: A SERIES ON DOMESTIC VIOLENCE

RISING STRONG: A SURVIVOR'S GUIDE TO THRIVING AFTER DOMESTIC VIOLENCE

Trient Press
3375 S Rainbow Blvd
#81710, SMB 13135
Las Vegas,NV 89180

Ordering Information:
Quantity sales. Special discounts are available on quantity purchases by corporations, associations, and others. For details, contact the publisher at the address above.
Orders by U.S. trade bookstores and wholesalers. Please contact Trient Press: Tel: (775) 996-3844; or visit www.trientpress.com.

Printed in the United States of America

Publisher's Cataloging-in-Publication data
Ruscsak, M.L.
A title of a book :Working for Your Dreams: Making this year your best year
ISBN
Paperback   978-1-955198-78-3
E-book   978-1-955198-79-0

"Embracing Empowerment: Overcoming Psychological Abuse"

"Finding Your Voice: Overcoming Verbal Abuse"

"Surviving and Thriving: Moving Past Physical Abuse"

"The Power of Forgiveness: Overcoming Emotional Abuse"

"Building a Better Future: Escaping Financial Abuse"

"Rising Above the Pain: Overcoming Sexual Abuse"

"The Path to Healing: Overcoming Stalking and Harassment"

"From Fear to Freedom: A Guide to Escaping Coercive

Control."

positive self-image

"From the darkness and ashes raises a warrior born to stand. From the trials of the past nothing can stop them from thriving. Beware the warrior forged in this fire for they are the ones destined to succeed. "

-Unknown

Domestic violence has been a constant presence in my life for far too long. I've seen it all - child abuse, family abuse, bullying, and finally, my own experience of being abused by my spouse. It's a journey full of ups and downs, twists and turns, and moments of pure terror and heartbreak. Despite all that I've been through, I'm still standing and I'm more determined than ever to help others who have experienced the same.

For years, I lived in fear and tried to protect myself by closing myself off from the world. This survival mechanism may have kept me safe, but it did nothing to help me thrive. It wasn't until I started to learn to trust again, recognize the red flags, and seek help that I began to see a path forward. I realized that the only way to truly heal and move on from my past experiences was to face them head-on. This was no easy feat, but with the help of friends, family, and professionals, I was able to take the first steps towards reclaiming my life.

I want to share my story with you because I know I'm not alone. Domestic violence takes many forms, and it affects us all in different ways. Some of us have seen it firsthand, while others have experienced it ourselves. Regardless of our individual experiences, we all share a common bond - a deep desire to heal and move forward. That's why I've written this book - to give you the tools and support you need to thrive after your own experience with domestic violence.

In the pages of this book, you'll find my story, along with the stories of others who have experienced domestic violence. You'll also find practical advice, tips, and exercises designed to help you heal, grow, and build a life that you deserve. Whether you're just starting your journey or you've been on it for a while, this book is for you.

One of the most important things I learned during my journey was the importance of self-care. It's all too easy to fall into the trap of neglecting ourselves when we're struggling to cope with trauma, but self-care is essential if we want to heal and thrive. In this book, you'll find guidance on how to prioritize self-care and make it a part of your a strong support system. This can be difficult when you're trying to heal, but having people in your life who understand what you're going through can make all the difference. In this book, you'll learn about the different types of support that are available to you, and how to build a network of friends and family who can help you on your journey.

Navigating the legal system can be one of the most daunting parts of recovering from domestic violence, but it's important to understand your rights and options. In this book, you'll find practical advice on how to work with law enforcement and the court system, as well as tips on preparing for trial and giving testimony. Whether you're looking for protection or seeking justice, this section will give you the tools you need to feel confident and in control.

Rebuilding your life after domestic violence can be a challenge, but it's also an opportunity to create something new and better. In this book, you'll find guidance on how to deal with financial stress and create a budget, how to find a job and create a stable source of income, and how to build self-esteem and a positive self-image. Whether you're starting from scratch or just looking to make changes, this book will provide you with the tools and resources you need to take control of your life and create a brighter future for yourself. You'll learn about the power of resilience and how to tap into it to overcome challenges and achieve your goals. You'll discover the importance of setting boundaries and learning to say "no" to toxic people and situations. And most importantly, you'll learn how to find the courage and strength to believe in yourself and your ability to create a life that is truly worth living.

PART 1
EXPLANATION OF THE PREVALENCE OF DOMESTIC VIOLENCE

PREVALENCE OF DOMESTIC VIOLENCE

Domestic violence is a pervasive and often hidden issue that affects millions of people around the world. While the specific numbers can vary depending on the source and definition used, one thing is clear: domestic violence is a widespread problem that touches the lives of far too many people. In this chapter, we'll explore the various forms that domestic violence can take, as well as the factors that contribute to its prevalence.

Domestic violence can take many forms, including physical, emotional, sexual, and psychological abuse. It can happen to anyone, regardless of age, gender, race, or socioeconomic status. Unfortunately, many people who experience domestic violence are reluctant to seek help, either out of fear of their abuser or because they believe that no one will believe them. This makes it difficult to accurately quantify the extent of the problem.

Despite this, there are some widely accepted estimates of the prevalence of domestic violence. According to the World Health Organization (WHO), one in three women worldwide will experience physical or sexual violence from an intimate partner in their lifetime. The National Domestic Violence Hotline reports that in the United States, an average of 20 people are physically abused by an intimate partner every minute. These are just a few of the staggering statistics that demonstrate the scale of the problem.

There are many factors that contribute to the prevalence of domestic violence. Some of the most common include poverty, substance abuse, mental health issues, and a history of trauma or abuse. The cycle of violence can be difficult to break, as perpetrators often use various forms of manipulation and control to keep their victims trapped in the relationship.

own journey of healing and recovery. Whether you're a survivor of domestic violence yourself or you're simply looking to understand the issue better, this chapter will provide you with a comprehensive overview of the prevalence of domestic violence and the factors that contribute to it.

JOURNAL EXERCISES

Reflect on your own experiences: Write down your thoughts and feelings about your own experiences with domestic violence, either as a survivor or as someone who has witnessed it.

_____

_____

_____

_____

_____

Explore the statistics: Research the statistics on domestic violence and reflect on what these numbers mean to you. How does it make you feel? What does it say about the state of our world?

_____

_____

_____

_____

_____

Consider the root causes: Consider the various factors that contribute to the prevalence of domestic violence, such as poverty, substance abuse, and mental health issues. Reflect on how these issues impact individuals and communities.

Connect with others: Connect with others who have experienced domestic violence and share your thoughts and feelings with them. This can be through support groups, online forums, or one-on-one conversations with trusted friends.

_____

_____

_____

_____

_____

Write a letter to your younger self: Write a letter to your younger self, before you experienced domestic violence, and offer words of encouragement and support.

_____

_____

_____

_____

_____

Visualize a world without domestic violence: Close your eyes and imagine a world in which domestic violence does not exist. What does this world look like? What does it feel like?

_____

_____

_____

Set a goal: Set a goal for yourself that relates to your recovery from domestic violence. This could be something as simple as reaching out to a support group or as ambitious as starting your own organization to help others.

_____

_____

_____

_____

_____

Express gratitude: Write down three things you are grateful for each day, even if they seem small. This exercise can help you focus on the positive and cultivate a sense of hope and resilience.

_____

_____

_____

_____

_____

Welcome to Chapter 2 of Rising Strong: A Survivor's Guide to Thriving After Domestic Violence. In this chapter, we'll explore the purpose of this book and why it's such an important resource for survivors of domestic violence.

Domestic violence can leave deep emotional scars and make it difficult to rebuild your life. It can be challenging to overcome the trauma of abuse and find a sense of stability and security. That's where this book comes in.

The purpose of Rising Strong is to provide you with the tools, resources, and support you need to thrive after domestic violence. We believe that every survivor has the capacity to heal and rebuild their life, and this book is designed to help you do just that.

In the pages of this book, you'll find information and guidance on a range of topics, including how to deal with financial stress, how to build self-esteem and a positive self-image, and how to find a job and create a stable source of income. We've also included journal exercises to help you reflect on your experiences, connect with others, and cultivate resilience and hope.

One of the key themes of this book is the importance of self-discovery and self-growth. We believe that, in order to heal and thrive after domestic violence, you need to understand and appreciate your own strengths, weaknesses, and potential. Through the journal exercises, you'll have the opportunity to explore your own feelings, thoughts, and experiences, and to identify areas in your life where you may need to make changes.

Another important theme of this book is the power of community. We believe that no one should have to face the challenges of domestic violence alone. By connecting with others who have had similar experiences, you can find comfort, support, and encouragement.

of domestic violence with the tools, resources, and support they need to heal, grow, and thrive. We believe that with the right guidance and support, every survivor has the capacity to build a happy, healthy, and fulfilling life. And we hope that this book will serve as a valuable resource on your journey to recovery and growth.

Places that you can look to seek help. As this book is intended to help as many people as possible I do not have the exact information per country. However here are places you can begin to seek help:

Hotlines: Many countries have hotlines that offer support and referrals to local resources for victims of domestic violence.

Shelters: Many countries have shelters or safe houses for victims of domestic violence, where they can stay and receive support and counseling.

Non-profit organizations: There are many non-profit organizations working to end domestic violence and provide support to victims. These organizations often offer counseling, legal advocacy, and other forms of support.

Government agencies: Many countries have government agencies responsible for addressing domestic violence. These agencies may provide support, resources, and legal assistance to victims.

Police: In many countries, police are trained to respond to domestic violence incidents and can provide protection and support to victims.

It's important to note that resources vary by country, so it's a good idea to do a search for "domestic violence resources [country name]" to find the specific resources available in your area. Additionally, if you or someone you know is in immediate danger, it's important to call emergency services such as 911.

As you begin your journey towards healing from the effects of domestic violence, it's important to remember that this road will not be easy. However, it's also important to keep in mind that it will get easier as you move forward. The journey ahead is not a straightforward path, but with the right tools and support, you can overcome the obstacles and find peace and happiness once again.

The first step on this journey is to ask for help. This can be a difficult step, but it's a critical one. Whether you reach out to a friend, a family member, a support group, or a professional, seeking help is a brave and important step towards healing.

As you move forward, you may encounter challenges and setbacks, but it's important to keep pushing forward. Your journey is unique, and the path you take will be different from others, but what is important is that you keep moving forward. Remember that you are not alone, and that there are people who care and want to help.

One of the most important things to keep in mind is that healing from domestic violence is a process, not an event. It may take time, and there will be ups and downs along the way. However, with persistence and determination, you can reach your goals and find the peace and happiness you deserve.

Throughout this journey, it's important to be patient with yourself and to focus on self-care. This may mean taking time for yourself, engaging in activities that bring you joy, and surrounding yourself with people who support and uplift you.

In conclusion, while the journey ahead may be difficult, it's also an opportunity for growth and healing. With the right support and resources, you can overcome the challenges and find the peace and happiness you deserve. Remember that each journey is different, but we are all here for each other, and together, we can rise strong.

positive aspects of your life and increase feelings of gratitude and joy.

2. Mindfulness meditation: Practicing mindfulness meditation can help calm the mind and reduce stress and anxiety. Start by setting aside a few minutes each day to focus on your breath and the present moment.

3. Affirmations: Write down positive affirmations and read them daily to help build self-esteem and confidence. Examples of affirmations include "I am strong," "I am worthy," and "I am capable."

4. Visualization: Close your eyes and visualize yourself in a peaceful and happy place. Use all your senses to immerse yourself in this place and focus on feeling relaxed and calm.

5. Self-care activities: Engage in activities that bring you joy and help you relax. This could be anything from taking a relaxing bath, to reading a book, to going for a walk in nature.

6. Expressing your emotions: Write down your feelings in a journal or talk to someone you trust about what you're going through. Expressing your emotions can help release feelings of anger, sadness, and frustration.

7. Connect with others: Reach out to friends, family, or a support group for emotional support and encouragement. Spending time with loved ones can help boost feelings of happiness and belonging.

8. Seek professional help: Consider seeing a therapist or counselor to work through the effects of domestic violence. A mental health professional can provide support and guidance to help you heal and move forward.

VIOLENCE

As a survivor of domestic violence, I want to share my story with you in the hopes that it will show you that you are not alone. I experienced violence and abuse at a young age, and it impacted me in ways I could never have imagined. From being locked in rooms, to being bullied, to facing negative relationships and thoughts of suicide, my journey through domestic violence was a difficult one. But through it all, I held on to hope and the belief that I could overcome my past and build a better future for myself.

In this chapter, I will share with you my personal story of surviving domestic violence and the steps I took to heal and thrive. I want to show you that, no matter how dark and hopeless your situation may seem, there is a light at the end of the tunnel. I want to offer you encouragement and inspire you to begin your own journey towards healing and self-discovery.

As a child, I witnessed my mother struggling with domestic violence, and I remember the fear and trauma that I experienced as a result. The nightmares and physical abuse I faced continued even after my mother left the relationship, and I felt trapped and powerless. The bullying and negative self-talk that I experienced in my teenage years only made things worse, and by the time I reached my twenties, I was struggling with thoughts of suicide.

However, I refused to let my past define me, and I started working on myself. I began to understand that the negative experiences I had faced were part of my past and had no power over my future. I made the decision to focus on my own healing and self-growth, and I slowly but surely began to rebuild my life.

In the following chapters, I want to share with you the lessons I learned along the way, the resources that helped me, and the tools I used to turn my life around. My hope is that by sharing my story, I can discovery, let's begin. Remember, you are not alone, and there is hope for a better tomorrow.

PART 2: UNDERSTANDING DOMESTIC VIOLENCE

violence can be a long and difficult one, but it is also filled with opportunities for growth and self-discovery.

As a survivor of domestic violence, you have undoubtedly experienced trauma and heartache that has left its mark on your life. However, it's important to remember that you are not defined by your past experiences. You have the strength and resilience to heal and move forward, and that is what this section is dedicated to helping you achieve.

In this chapter, we will be exploring the various forms of domestic violence, including physical, emotional, sexual, and financial abuse. You will learn about the warning signs of domestic violence, and how to identify them in your own relationships. Additionally, we will be discussing the long-term effects of domestic violence on survivors and how it can impact their lives years after leaving the abusive relationship.

The road to healing may not be easy, but it is possible. By understanding the root causes of domestic violence, you can take the first step towards healing and reclaiming your life. So, let's begin this journey together and work towards a brighter future filled with love, hope, and happiness.

[illegible] and self-discovery.

Domestic violence is a complex issue that can take many forms. It is a pattern of behavior used by one person to maintain power and control over another person in an intimate relationship. This type of violence can take many different forms, including physical, sexual, emotional, and psychological abuse. In order to fully understand the nature and scope of domestic violence, it is important to examine each type of abuse in more detail.

Physical abuse refers to any intentional use of physical force against another person. This can include hitting, punching, pushing, kicking, or using weapons to cause physical harm. Physical abuse can also include acts of violence that result in injury, such as choking or strangling. In some cases, physical abuse can lead to serious injury or even death.

Sexual abuse refers to any non-consensual sexual act, including rape, sexual assault, and other forms of sexual violence. Sexual abuse can be physical or emotional, and can take many different forms. It is a form of violence that can have lasting effects on a person's health, relationships, and overall well-being.

Emotional abuse refers to any non-physical behavior that is intended to harm another person's emotions or psychological well-being. This can include verbal abuse, such as name-calling or belittling, as well as psychological manipulation and control. Emotional abuse can be just as damaging as physical abuse, and can have long-lasting effects on a person's mental health and self-esteem.

Psychological abuse refers to any behavior that is intended to harm another person's mental or emotional state. This can include gaslighting, threats, manipulation, and other forms of psychological control. Psychological abuse can have a profound impact on a person's self-esteem, mental health, and overall well-being.

It is important to recognize that domestic violence can take many different forms, and that each type of abuse can have serious consequences for the victim. Whether you are experiencing physical,

Warning signs that a person may be in an abusive relationship:

✧ Controlling behavior: Does your partner control what you do, who you see or talk to, or where you go?

✧ Isolation: Has your partner stopped you from spending time with family and friends or pursuing activities that you enjoy?

✧ Threats: Has your partner threatened you, your children, pets, or other loved ones?

✧ Physical violence: Has your partner ever hit, slapped, pushed, or kicked you?

✧ Verbal abuse: Does your partner call you names, put you down, or make you feel bad about yourself?

✧ Economic control: Does your partner control the money and prevent you from having access to financial resources?

✧ Sexual violence: Has your partner ever forced you to have sex or engage in sexual acts against your will?

✧ Stalking: Has your partner followed you, monitored your phone or computer, or shown up at your workplace or home unexpectedly?

✧ Using weapons: Has your partner ever threatened you with a weapon or actually used one against you?

It's important to remember that abuse can take many forms and may not always be physical. If you're experiencing any of these warning signs, it's important to reach out for help.

Domestic violence is not just a physical act, but it also takes a toll on the mental, emotional, and psychological well-being of individuals and families. The impact of domestic violence can last for years, even long after the abusive relationship has ended. Understanding the effects of domestic violence is crucial to the healing process and moving forward towards a better future.

For individuals who have experienced domestic violence, it can be difficult to trust others, especially intimate partners. It can lead to feelings of low self-esteem, shame, guilt, and a negative self-image. This can cause significant emotional distress, and make it difficult to form healthy relationships in the future.

The impact of domestic violence can also lead to a range of mental health issues, such as anxiety, depression, and post-traumatic stress disorder (PTSD). These conditions can make it difficult to function in daily life, and can also increase the risk of substance abuse and other negative coping mechanisms.

Domestic violence also affects families and children, who are often witnesses to the abuse. Children who grow up in homes where there is domestic violence are more likely to experience behavioral and emotional problems, and may also be at increased risk for becoming victims of abuse themselves later in life.

Despite these challenges, it's important to remember that healing is possible, and that there is hope for a better future. The journey towards recovery can be difficult, but with support from family, friends, and professionals, individuals and families can find ways to heal and rebuild their lives. In this chapter, we will explore the impact of domestic violence on individuals and families, and provide tips for healing and recovery.

thoughts that come up as you think about this topic.

_____

_____

_____

_____

_____

Identifying Trauma: Write down any traumatic experiences you've had as a result of domestic violence. Be specific and descriptive, and take time to process your emotions as you write.

_____

_____

_____

_____

_____

Family Tree: Draw a family tree and reflect on how domestic violence has impacted each family member. Write down any observations or insights you have about how the trauma has affected each person.

_____

_____

_____

_____

_____

_____

_____

_____

_____

_____

Support System: Write about the support system you have in place to help you deal with the impact of domestic violence. Who are the people you turn to for help and comfort? How have they helped you through this difficult time?

_____

_____

_____

_____

_____

Coping Mechanisms: Write about any coping mechanisms you've used to deal with the impact of domestic violence. What works for you and what doesn't? How have these coping mechanisms impacted your mental and emotional well-being?

_____

_____

_____

_____

_____

_____

_____

_____

_____

_____

Gratitude: Write about what you are grateful for in your life. How does focusing on gratitude help you deal with the impact of domestic violence?

_____

_____

_____

_____

_____

These exercises can help individuals process their experiences and emotions related to domestic violence and provide a foundation for continued healing and growth.

Leaving a relationship marked by domestic violence is never an easy decision, but it is an important one for both personal safety and long-term healing. However, for many survivors, the process of leaving can feel overwhelming, confusing, and even impossible. This chapter will explore the reasons why it's difficult to leave, and what you can do to help break the cycle of abuse.

The cycle of abuse is a pattern that often occurs in abusive relationships, characterized by alternating periods of tension and abuse followed by periods of calm, apologies, and even affection. This cycle can make it difficult for survivors to leave, as they may feel confused, scared, or even hopeful that their partner will change. But the cycle of abuse is often repeated, and it can be difficult to escape without help and support.

One of the reasons why it's difficult to leave an abusive relationship is fear. Fear of retribution, fear of being alone, fear of financial hardship, and fear of being unable to protect oneself and one's loved ones can all keep a person trapped in an abusive relationship. Moreover, abuse can take many forms and can be psychological, emotional, physical, and sexual. This can make it difficult for survivors to recognize that they are in an abusive relationship and to find the courage to leave.

Another reason why it's difficult to leave an abusive relationship is the emotional bond that can develop between the abuser and the survivor. An abuser may use a variety of tactics, such as isolation, manipulation, and control, to create a strong emotional bond with the survivor, making it difficult for them to leave. Additionally, survivors may feel a sense of shame or guilt for staying in an abusive relationship, which can make it even harder for them to leave.

Despite these challenges, there is hope. With the right support and resources, survivors can leave an abusive relationship and begin the journey towards healing and recovery. The goal of this chapter is to

JOURNAL EXERCISES

Write down the reasons why you have stayed in your abusive relationship up until this point.

_____

_____

_____

_____

_____

Consider what factors may have contributed to your fear of leaving the relationship.

_____

_____

_____

_____

_____

Reflect on any emotional bonds you may have with your abuser and how they may be affecting your ability to leave.

_____

_____

_____

_____

_____

Write a letter to yourself, offering encouragement and hope as you embark on this journey of leaving the abuse behind.

_____

Make a list of people or resources you can turn to for help and support as you work towards leaving the cycle of abuse.

_____

_____

_____

_____

_____

In conclusion, understanding domestic violence is crucial to breaking the cycle of abuse and moving towards a healthy, safe and fulfilling life. While it can be difficult to recognize the warning signs and leave an abusive situation, it is important to remember that you are not alone and that there is help available. The impact of domestic violence on individuals and families can be devastating, but it is also possible to heal from these experiences and create a better future.

In this part of the book, we have explored the definition and types of domestic violence, the warning signs of abuse, and the cycle of abuse that can make it difficult to leave. By becoming aware of these patterns and the impact they have, you can take the first steps towards reclaiming your life and creating a better future.

It is important to remember that healing and growth take time and effort, but it is possible to overcome the effects of domestic violence and find peace and happiness. With the right support and tools, you can overcome the challenges and reclaim your life, creating a brighter future full of hope and positivity.

JOURNAL EXERCISES

Here are some journal exercises that can be inspiring and give hope for those affected by domestic violence:

learned and the challenges you have overcome.

_____

_____

_____

_____

_____

Gratitude list: Write a list of things you are grateful for in your life. Focus on the positive aspects of your life and reflect on the strength and resilience you have shown so far.

_____

_____

_____

_____

_____

Future vision: Write about your hopes and dreams for the future. What kind of life do you want to create for yourself and your loved ones? How will you make this vision a reality?

_____

_____

_____

_____

_____

_____

_____

_____

_____

_____

Support system: Write about the people in your life who provide you with support and encouragement. Reflect on the ways in which their support has helped you to heal and grow, and consider ways you can show your appreciation for them.

_____

_____

_____

_____

_____

Healing visualization: Close your eyes and imagine yourself in a peaceful, healing environment. Visualize yourself being surrounded by love and support, and imagine yourself feeling happy, healthy, and free from the effects of domestic violence. Write about your visualization and how it makes you feel.

_____

_____

_____

_____

_____

PART 3 COPING WITH TRAUMA

move forward with hope and positivity. In this chapter, we will cover three key areas: the recognition of symptoms of trauma, the importance of self-care and self-compassion, and the benefits of seeking professional support for trauma recovery.

Recognizing the Symptoms of Trauma

The first step in the process of healing from trauma is to recognize the symptoms. Trauma can manifest in a variety of ways, including physical symptoms like headaches or insomnia, as well as emotional symptoms such as anxiety or depression. Understanding the signs and symptoms of trauma is an important part of the healing process and will help you take the steps needed to start your journey towards recovery.

The Importance of Self-Care and Self-Compassion

In addition to recognizing the symptoms of trauma, it is equally important to prioritize self-care and self-compassion. This means taking care of your physical, emotional, and mental well-being by engaging in activities that bring you joy and comfort, and practicing self-compassion by speaking kindly to yourself and embracing your own imperfections. Self-care and self-compassion are essential tools in the process of healing from trauma, and can help you maintain a positive outlook on life and a sense of hope for the future.

Seeking Professional Support for Trauma Recovery

Finally, seeking professional support is an important step in the process of healing from trauma. This can include therapy, counseling, or support groups. Having a trained professional to talk to can provide a safe space for you to process your feelings and experiences, and can help you work through any lingering negative emotions or behaviors. It is important to remember that seeking help is a sign of strength and courage, and it is never too late to start your journey towards healing.

support needed to help you on your journey, and we encourage you to continue reading and exploring the strategies and techniques outlined in this book.

Trauma can leave a lasting impact on an individual, causing physical and emotional distress.

It can be difficult to identify the symptoms of trauma, especially if you're trying to keep them hidden from the rest of the world.

Common physical symptoms of trauma include headaches, stomach aches, and difficulty sleeping.

Emotional symptoms of trauma include feelings of fear, anger, guilt, shame, and depression.

Trauma can also lead to feelings of detachment, disconnection, and a sense of being stuck in the past.

People who have experienced trauma may struggle with trust issues, which can make it difficult to form healthy relationships.

Trauma can also cause anxiety, panic attacks, and an increased startle response.

Some individuals may experience flashbacks or recurring memories of the traumatic event, leading to a sense of re-living the event.

It's important to recognize the symptoms of trauma, as this is the first step in seeking help and finding healing.

If you're struggling with the symptoms of trauma, don't be afraid to reach out to friends, family, or a mental health professional for support. With the right resources and support, it's possible to overcome the effects of trauma and live a fulfilling, happy life.

The Lasting Impact of Trauma

Trauma can have a profound impact on an individual, leaving both physical and emotional scars that can last a lifetime. It is not uncommon for those who have experienced trauma to feel overwhelmed, anxious, and disconnected from the world around them. Trauma can also manifest itself in a variety of physical symptoms, such as headaches, fatigue, and trouble sleeping.

The Nature of Trauma

Trauma is a natural response to a traumatic event or series of events that causes the individual to feel threatened and in danger. This

The Physical Symptoms of Trauma

Trauma can cause a variety of physical symptoms, including headaches, fatigue, trouble sleeping, and more. These symptoms can be difficult to manage and can take a toll on an individual's mental and emotional well-being. In some cases, the physical symptoms of trauma can even lead to further complications, such as chronic pain or autoimmune disorders.

The Emotional Symptoms of Trauma

In addition to physical symptoms, trauma can also have a lasting impact on an individual's emotional well-being. It is not uncommon for those who have experienced trauma to feel overwhelmed, anxious, and disconnected from the world around them. They may also experience feelings of guilt, shame, and fear, and they may struggle to form healthy relationships or maintain close bonds with loved ones.

The Importance of Recognizing Trauma

Recognizing the symptoms of trauma is an important step in the healing process. By understanding the physical and emotional impact of trauma, individuals can take steps to manage their symptoms and find support. It is also important to recognize that everyone's experience with trauma is unique, and that there is no "right" way to cope with the aftermath of a traumatic event.

The Stigma of Trauma

Despite its widespread impact, there is still a stigma surrounding trauma and its aftermath. Many individuals who have experienced trauma may feel ashamed or embarrassed to speak up about their experiences, which can prevent them from seeking the support they need to heal. It is important to remember that trauma is a natural response to a traumatic event, and that there is no shame in seeking help.

along the way, but with the right tools and support, it is possible to overcome and find peace. This can include seeking professional help, connecting with others who have gone through similar experiences, and engaging in self-care and self-compassion practices.

Seeking Professional Support

Professional support can be a valuable resource for those seeking to heal from trauma. Therapists, counselors, and other mental health professionals can help individuals to process their experiences and find healthy coping mechanisms. They can also help to address any underlying mental health conditions that may be contributing to the symptoms of trauma.

Finding a Support System

In addition to professional support, connecting with others who have gone through similar experiences can be a valuable part of the healing process. Whether through therapy groups, support groups, or simply reaching out to friends and family, it is important to have a support system in place as you work to heal from trauma.

JOURNAL EXERCISES

Here are some journal exercises for exploring the lasting effects of trauma:

Write a letter to your trauma: In this exercise, take some time to reflect on how trauma has impacted you and write a letter to your trauma. You can express your feelings and thoughts about the trauma and its effects on your life.

_____

_____

Reflect on triggers: Write down a list of things that trigger memories of your trauma. Reflect on how each trigger makes you feel and what you can do to manage these feelings.

_____

_____

_____

_____

_____

Mindful breathing: Take a few minutes to focus on your breathing. As you breathe in, imagine breathing in calm and peace. As you breathe out, imagine breathing out stress and anxiety. Repeat this process until you feel more relaxed and centered.

_____

_____

_____

_____

_____

Gratitude practice: Each day, write down three things you are grateful for. Reflect on how these things bring joy and happiness into your life, even in the midst of difficult memories and emotions related to your trauma.

_____

_____

_____

_____

_____

_____

_____

_____

_____

_____

Write about your strengths: Take some time to reflect on the strengths and qualities that have helped you overcome your trauma. Write about these strengths and how you can continue to use them to heal and move forward.

_____

_____

_____

_____

_____

Affirmations: Write positive affirmations that reflect your values and goals for healing. Repeat these affirmations to yourself each day, reminding yourself of your worth and strength.

_____

_____

_____

_____

_____

Art therapy: Use art to express your feelings and experiences related to your trauma. This can include drawing, painting, or collaging.

_____

_____

_____

Express your feelings: Write about the emotions you are experiencing related to your trauma. This can be a cathartic experience, helping you to release feelings of anger, sadness, or fear.

_____

_____

_____

_____

_____

Focus on self-care: Write about self-care activities you can engage in to help you manage the effects of your trauma. This can include things like exercise, meditation, or spending time with loved ones. Reflect on how each activity makes you feel and what benefits you experience from each one.

_____

_____

_____

_____

_____

Understanding the Hidden Symptoms of Trauma

It can be difficult to identify the symptoms of trauma, especially if you're trying to keep them hidden from the rest of the world. The

Exercises:

Reflect on your physical and emotional well-being. Make a list of any symptoms or changes that you have noticed since experiencing trauma.

_____

_____

_____

_____

_____

Consider how your experiences may have affected your daily life. Have you been withdrawing from friends and family, or are you having difficulty sleeping or concentrating?

_____

_____

_____

_____

_____

Write down any negative self-talk or beliefs that you have been telling yourself since the traumatic event. This could be things like, "I'm not good enough," or "I will never feel happy again."

_____

_____

_____

_____

_____

_____

_____

_____

_____

_____

Reflect on how your relationships have been affected by your experiences with trauma. Have you been withdrawing from friends and family, or have you noticed any changes in your intimate relationships?

_____

_____

_____

_____

_____

Take time each day to focus on self-care and self-compassion. This could include things like journaling, practicing mindfulness, or engaging in activities that bring you joy and peace.

_____

_____

_____

_____

_____

Seek support from a trusted friend, family member, or professional therapist. Talking about your experiences and receiving support can help you to process and heal from the effects of trauma.

_____

_____

_____

the healing process. With time, patience, and the right support, you can overcome the lasting effects of trauma and find peace.

_____
_____
_____
_____
_____

The Physical Toll of Trauma: Understanding the Physical Symptoms

Trauma can manifest itself in many different ways, and one of the most common ways is through physical symptoms. These symptoms can range from headaches and stomach aches to difficulty sleeping. They may seem small or insignificant, but they can be a sign of something much deeper and more serious. Understanding these physical symptoms is an important step in recognizing and coping with trauma.

Some common physical symptoms of trauma include:

✧ Headaches - Trauma can cause tension in the body, which can lead to headaches and migraines.

✧ Stomach aches - Trauma can cause physical tension in the body, leading to digestive problems like stomach aches and nausea.

✧ Difficulty sleeping - Trauma can cause anxiety, leading to difficulty sleeping and even insomnia.

✧ Fatigue - Trauma can take a toll on the body and mind, causing exhaustion and fatigue.

you need to heal.

JOURNAL EXERCISES:

Write down any physical symptoms you have been experiencing and how long you have had them.

_____

_____

_____

_____

_____

Reflect on how trauma may have caused or contributed to these physical symptoms.

_____

_____

_____

_____

_____

Write down some self-care activities that you can do to help manage these physical symptoms.

_____

_____

_____

_____

_____

Trauma can take a heavy toll on an individual's emotions, leading to feelings of detachment, disconnection, and a sense of being stuck in the past. This can cause a person to feel isolated, disconnected from others, and unable to move forward with their life. These feelings are normal and common among those who have experienced trauma, but they can also be debilitating and prevent a person from leading a fulfilling life.

It's important to understand that these feelings are not permanent and can be addressed with the right support and resources. In this section, we will explore the emotional effects of trauma and provide practical exercises for overcoming them.

Examples:

✧ A person may feel like they are constantly on edge and unable to fully relax or enjoy life.

✧ They may feel emotionally numb, disconnected from their own feelings and those of others.

✧ They may have trouble forming or maintaining close relationships, either with friends or loved ones.

✧ They may find themselves constantly re-experiencing traumatic events in their mind, and feel like they can't move on from the past.

✧ They may also feel a sense of guilt or shame, believing that they should have done something to prevent the traumatic events from happening.

✧ These are just a few examples of the types of feelings and experiences that can result from trauma. By highlighting these

Write down the feelings you associate with the trauma you have experienced.

_____

_____

_____

_____

_____

Reflect on any times when you have felt detached, disconnected, or stuck in the past. What were the circumstances that led to these feelings?

_____

_____

_____

_____

_____

Write a letter to your inner child, offering comfort and reassurance that you are safe now and that you will take care of them.

_____

_____

_____

_____

_____

Write a list of activities that bring you joy and make you feel connected to the present moment. Try to engage in these activities regularly.

_____

Reach out to someone you trust and share your feelings with them. It can be a friend, family member, or therapist. Talking about your experiences can help you feel less alone and more connected.

_____

_____

_____

_____

_____

Breaking the Cycle of Distrust: Overcoming Trust Issues After Trauma

Trauma can leave deep scars on an individual, not just physically, but emotionally and mentally as well. One of the common aftermaths of trauma is a struggle with trust issues, which can make it challenging to form healthy relationships with others. Trust is an essential component of any relationship, and without it, one may feel anxious, paranoid, and disconnected from the world around them.

The loss of trust can be a result of a traumatic experience where an individual's trust was violated or shattered. This can make it difficult to trust anyone, even those who have not caused harm. Trust issues can also stem from feelings of abandonment, betrayal, or neglect, making it challenging to open up to others and form meaningful connections.

It's important to understand that trust issues are a normal response to trauma and that they can be overcome with time and effort. Here are some journal exercises to help you work through your trust issues and build healthier relationships:

Reflect on past relationships: Write down the relationships you have had in the past, both positive and negative. Consider how each feelings and thoughts that arise in these situations.

Practice self-compassion: Write a letter to yourself acknowledging the difficulties you have faced and expressing compassion and understanding towards yourself. Remind yourself that it's okay to feel distrust and that you are worthy of love and trust.

Rebuild trust: Write down steps you can take to rebuild trust in yourself and others. This can include therapy, talking to a trusted friend or loved one, or participating in activities that bring you joy and build confidence.

By engaging in these exercises, you can work through your trust issues and build healthier relationships. Remember, it's a journey, and progress may be slow, but with persistence and self-care, you can overcome the challenges and find peace and happiness.

Short Stories for both positive and negative effects of not trusting due to trauma:

Positive Effect:
Once upon a time, there was a woman named Sarah who had experienced trauma in her past. Despite this, she was determined to overcome and heal. She sought therapy and learned about the effects of trauma on her life, including her trust issues. With the help of her therapist and supportive friends, Sarah was able to work through her trust issues and form healthy relationships. She found happiness in her relationships and felt a sense of connection and love.

Negative Effect:
Once upon a time, there was a man named John who had experienced trauma in his past. He struggled with trust issues, causing him to push away those who cared about him. He refused to seek help and instead isolated himself from the world. He felt lonely and disconnected, and his relationships suffered as a result. John realized

Trauma can have a significant impact on the body, causing physical symptoms such as headaches, stomach aches, and difficulty sleeping. These physical symptoms can be a sign that you're struggling with the aftermath of a traumatic event. If you're experiencing any of these symptoms, it's important to seek help and support from a mental health professional.

JOURNAL EXERCISE

Take some time to reflect on your physical symptoms and any changes you've noticed since experiencing trauma. Write down any questions or concerns you have and make a plan to talk to a mental health professional about them.

_____

_____

_____

_____

_____

The Emotional Symptoms of Trauma

Trauma can also affect your emotional wellbeing, leading to feelings of detachment, disconnection, and a sense of being stuck in the past. People who have experienced trauma may also struggle with trust issues, making it difficult to form healthy relationships. If you're experiencing any of these emotional symptoms, it's important to seek help and support.

JOURNAL EXERCISE

Take some time to reflect on your emotional symptoms and how they may be related to your experience of trauma. Write down any

_____

_____

_____

_____

The Impact of Trauma on Mental Health

Trauma can cause a range of mental health issues, including anxiety, panic attacks, and an increased startle response. Some individuals may experience flashbacks or recurring memories of the traumatic event, leading to a sense of re-living the event. These symptoms can be overwhelming and debilitating, but with the right support, it's possible to overcome them.

JOURNAL EXERCISE

Take some time to reflect on any changes you've noticed in your mental health since experiencing trauma. Write down any questions or concerns you have and make a plan to talk to a mental health professional about them.

_____

_____

_____

_____

_____

Seeking Help for Trauma Recovery

It's important to recognize the symptoms of trauma and seek help as soon as possible. If you're struggling with the effects of trauma, don't be afraid to reach out to friends, family, or a mental health professional

Take some time to reflect on the support systems you have in your life, such as friends and family, and think about how they can help you on your journey to recovery. Make a plan to reach out to them and seek their support.

_____

_____

_____

_____

_____

Conclusion:

In this chapter, we have explored the symptoms of trauma and the importance of recognizing them. Remember, you are not alone and with the right support and resources, it's possible to overcome the effects of trauma and find healing. Take the steps necessary to seek help and support, and never be afraid to reach out to friends, family, or a mental health professional for help. You have the strength and resilience to overcome any obstacle, and with time and support, you can live a fulfilling, happy life.

Definition of self-care and self-compassion
Explanation of how self-care and self-compassion relate to trauma recovery
Overview of the benefits of incorporating self-care and self-compassion into your life

II. Understanding Self-Care

What is self-care
Why self-care is important
Examples of self-care activities

III. The Benefits of Self-Care

Improving physical health
Reducing stress and anxiety
Enhancing emotional well-being
Improving relationships

IV. Understanding Self-Compassion

What is self-compassion
Why self-compassion is important
How to cultivate self-compassion
V. The Benefits of Self-Compassion

Improving self-worth and self-esteem
Decreasing negative self-talk and criticism
Enhancing resilience and coping skills
Improving overall well-being

VI. Practical Tips for Incorporating Self-Care and Self-Compassion into Your Life

Making time for self-care and self-compassion activities

Recap of the importance of self-care and self-compassion

Encouragement to make self-care and self-compassion a priority in your life

Final thoughts on the journey to healing and thriving after trauma.

journey after trauma. As survivors of domestic violence, it's common to experience feelings of guilt, shame, and self-blame, which can make it difficult to take care of ourselves. However, taking care of ourselves is essential to our overall well-being and our ability to heal and recover from the effects of trauma. In this chapter, we will explore the different aspects of self-care, the importance of self-compassion, and how these tools can help us on the path to healing and recovery. By the end of this chapter, we hope to empower you with the knowledge and inspiration to make self-care a priority in your life.

The Importance of Self-Care and Self-Compassion

I. Definition of Self-Care and Self-Compassion
A. Self-care defined as intentional actions to promote physical, emotional, and mental well-being
B. Self-compassion defined as being kind and understanding towards oneself, especially during difficult times

II. Relating Self-Care and Self-Compassion to Trauma Recovery
A. Trauma can leave individuals feeling overwhelmed, vulnerable, and in need of care
B. Incorporating self-care and self-compassion can provide comfort, support, and a sense of control during the healing process

III. Overview of the Benefits of Incorporating Self-Care and Self-Compassion
A. Improving physical health by reducing stress and promoting relaxation
B. Enhancing mental health by reducing feelings of anxiety, depression, and guilt
C. Building resilience and emotional stability, allowing individuals to better cope with challenges
D. Improving self-esteem and body image, leading to increased confidence and self-worth
E. Strengthening relationships by improving communication, reducing conflict, and promoting understanding

our daily routine can have a profound impact on our mental and physical health, helping us to thrive and find peace in the wake of trauma.

Section II: Understanding Self-Care

What is Self-Care
Self-care is an integral part of your overall health and well-being. It's all about taking the time to focus on your physical, emotional, and mental needs, and taking care of yourself.

Why Self-Care is Important
Self-care is important because it helps you to recharge and maintain a positive state of mind. It also helps to reduce stress, increase resilience, and improve your overall quality of life. For those who have experienced trauma, self-care is especially important as it can help you to manage the symptoms of trauma and promote healing.

Examples of Self-Care Activities
Self-care can come in many forms, including physical, emotional, and mental activities. Some examples of physical self-care activities include exercise, eating a healthy diet, and getting enough sleep. Emotional self-care activities include practicing gratitude, journaling, and talking to a trusted friend. Mental self-care activities include meditating, practicing mindfulness, and engaging in creative pursuits. The key to successful self-care is to find what works best for you and make it a regular part of your routine.

Section III: The Benefits of Self-Care

Self-care is one of the most powerful tools you have at your disposal when it comes to coping with trauma and promoting recovery. By prioritizing your own well-being and taking care of yourself, you can reap a number of powerful benefits that can improve your physical health, reduce stress and anxiety, enhance your emotional well-being, and even improve your relationships with others.

Reducing Stress and Anxiety: Life after trauma can be incredibly stressful and anxiety-inducing, but self-care can help you manage these feelings and reduce their impact on your life. Whether it's through meditation, journaling, or simply taking a relaxing bath, self-care can help you find calm and peace.

Enhancing Emotional Well-Being: One of the most important benefits of self-care is that it can help you cultivate a sense of emotional well-being. By engaging in activities that bring you joy and fulfillment, you can boost your mood and build resilience against the effects of trauma.

Improving Relationships: Finally, self-care can also have a positive impact on your relationships with others. When you prioritize your own well-being, you become a more confident, centered, and emotionally available person, which can help you connect with others in meaningful ways.

So, whether you're dealing with the aftermath of trauma or simply looking for ways to improve your overall health and happiness, don't underestimate the power of self-care. Incorporating self-care activities into your daily routine can help you find peace, happiness, and a renewed sense of purpose, no matter what challenges you may be facing.

Here are a few exercises related to self-care that can enhance the benefits of self-care in reducing stress and anxiety, improving physical health, enhancing emotional well-being, and improving relationships:

✧ Daily Gratitude Practice: Write down three things you are grateful for every day, this can help shift focus to the positive aspects of life and enhance overall well-being.

pull one out when you need a quick pick-me-up.

✧ Affirmations: Write positive affirmations about yourself and repeat them daily. This can help build confidence and self-compassion.

✧ Self-Care Time Block: Schedule time in your week for self-care activities, like taking a relaxing bath, getting a massage, or simply reading a book.

✧ Positive Social Interactions: Spend time with positive people who make you feel good. This can help enhance relationships and emotional well-being.

✧ Exercise: Incorporating physical activity into your routine can help improve physical health, reduce stress, and enhance overall well-being.

✧ Mindful Eating: Pay attention to the food you eat and the experience of eating. This can help you better understand your eating habits and improve physical health.

IV. Understanding Self-Compassion

Self-compassion refers to treating oneself with kindness, care, and understanding. It involves recognizing that everyone makes mistakes, experiences difficulties, and feels pain and suffering. Rather than harsh self-criticism and judgment, self-compassion encourages us to extend compassion to ourselves, just as we would to others.

Why is self-compassion important?

Self-compassion has been shown to have a number of benefits, including reducing stress, anxiety, and depression, improving emotional well-being, and enhancing resilience. For individuals who have experienced trauma, self-compassion can play a crucial role in the

Here are a few tips for cultivating self-compassion in your life:

Practice mindfulness: Pay attention to your thoughts, feelings, and physical sensations in a non-judgmental way.

Treat yourself with kindness: Instead of criticizing yourself for mistakes or shortcomings, talk to yourself as you would to a close friend.

Cultivate gratitude: Take time to reflect on the things in your life that you are grateful for, and focus on these positive aspects of your life.

Practice self-care: Engage in activities that bring you joy and relaxation, such as exercise, reading, or spending time with friends and family.

Seek support: Reach out to friends, family, or a mental health professional for support and encouragement when needed.

V. The Benefits of Self-Compassion

Self-compassion can have a profound impact on our mental and emotional health. Here are a few of the key benefits of developing self-compassion:

Improving self-worth and self-esteem: When we practice self-compassion, we learn to treat ourselves with kindness, understanding, and empathy. This helps us to develop a more positive self-image and feel better about ourselves.

Decreasing negative self-talk and criticism: Self-compassion encourages us to speak to ourselves in a more gentle, supportive way. This helps to decrease the frequency and severity of negative self-talk and self-criticism.

Improving overall well-being: When we develop self-compassion, we experience greater feelings of happiness, contentment, and peace. Our relationships improve, our stress levels decrease, and we feel more fulfilled in life.

Incorporating self-compassion into your life can have a profound impact on your well-being. By treating yourself with kindness, understanding, and empathy, you can overcome the lasting effects of trauma and reclaim control of your life.

Practical Tips for Incorporating Self-Care and Self-Compassion into Your Life

Making Time for Self-Care and Self-Compassion Activities: It's important to carve out time for self-care and self-compassion activities, even if it's just a few minutes a day. This can help you prioritize your well-being and reduce stress and anxiety.

Incorporating Self-Care and Self-Compassion into Your Daily Routine: You can make self-care and self-compassion a regular part of your life by incorporating them into your daily routine. For example, you could start each day with a few minutes of mindfulness meditation, or take a break from work to go for a walk or do some yoga.

Surrounding Yourself with Supportive People: Surrounding yourself with supportive friends and family can help boost your self-care and self-compassion practices. You can also join a support group, where you can connect with others who understand what you're going through.

Seeking Professional Help If Needed: If you're struggling with the effects of trauma and finding it difficult to incorporate self-care and self-compassion into your life, don't be afraid to seek professional help. A mental health professional can provide you with the support and

In conclusion, self-care and self-compassion are key components of trauma recovery. By understanding the importance of self-care and self-compassion, incorporating them into your daily routine, and seeking support when needed, you can improve your physical and emotional health, enhance your well-being, and overcome the effects of trauma. Remember to be patient with yourself and be kind to yourself, as healing takes time and effort.

Exercises:

✧ Self-Care and Self-Compassion Check-In: Take a few moments each day to check in with yourself and assess your self-care and self-compassion practices. Write down what you did for self-care today and how it made you feel. Similarly, write down instances where you were kind and compassionate towards yourself.

✧ Self-Care Plan: Create a self-care plan that outlines specific activities you will do each day to take care of yourself physically, mentally, and emotionally. This can include things like exercise, meditation, spending time with loved ones, or doing a hobby you enjoy.

✧ Gratitude Practice: Each day, write down three things you are grateful for and how they bring joy and comfort to your life. This exercise can help cultivate feelings of self-compassion and gratitude.

✧ Positive Affirmations: Write a list of positive affirmations that reflect your values, strengths, and qualities. Read these affirmations daily and focus on internalizing them.

✧ Kind Self-Talk: When you notice negative self-talk, take a moment to pause and reframe your thoughts with kindness and compassion. Write down instances where you practice kind self-talk and how it impacted your mood and overall well-being.

It takes great strength and courage to face the aftermath of a traumatic experience and begin the journey of recovery. Whether it's physical, emotional, or both, trauma can leave a lasting impact that affects every aspect of your life. You may feel overwhelmed, alone, and unsure of where to turn for help. But the good news is, you don't have to go through it alone. There is professional support available to assist you in your healing process and help you regain a sense of control over your life. This chapter will explore the benefits of seeking professional support for trauma recovery and what you can expect from the process.

I. Understanding the Benefits of Professional Support

Improved physical and emotional well-being
Increased sense of control and empowerment
Opportunities for personal growth and development
Increased likelihood of successful, long-term recovery

II. Types of Professional Support for Trauma Recovery

Therapists and Counselors
Psychologists and Psychiatrists
Group Therapy and Support Groups
Medication and Medical Treatments

III. Finding the Right Professional Support for You

Considerations when selecting a therapist or counselor
Understanding the different approaches to therapy
The importance of a good fit and rapport with your therapist

IV. Taking the First Step in Seeking Professional Support

Overcoming fear and shame associated with seeking help
Making the decision to seek professional support

The importance of prioritizing self-care and self-compassion in the process of trauma recovery

Encouragement to take action and seek professional support if needed.

I. Understanding the Benefits of Professional Support

Trauma can have a profound and lasting impact on our lives, affecting us in ways that can be difficult to understand and manage on our own. Fortunately, there is help available, and seeking professional support can be a vital step on the road to recovery. In this section, we'll explore the benefits of working with a mental health professional to overcome the effects of trauma.

Improved Physical and Emotional Well-Being

One of the most important benefits of seeking professional support is improved physical and emotional well-being. Trauma can take a toll on our bodies and minds, leading to a range of symptoms such as headaches, stomach aches, anxiety, and depression. Working with a mental health professional can help you manage these symptoms, reducing your overall stress levels and improving your overall health.

Increased Sense of Control and Empowerment

In the aftermath of trauma, it can be easy to feel overwhelmed and powerless. Seeking professional support can help you regain a sense of control and empower you to take steps towards recovery. With the help of a trained mental health professional, you'll learn new coping skills and strategies for managing the effects of trauma, giving you the tools you need to take control of your life.

opportunity to explore your thoughts and feelings, identify patterns and behaviors that may be contributing to your trauma, and develop new insights into yourself and your experiences. This can help you grow as a person, leading to greater self-awareness, self-acceptance, and a stronger sense of purpose.

Increased Likelihood of Successful, Long-Term Recovery

Finally, seeking professional support can increase the likelihood of successful, long-term recovery from trauma. Working with a mental health professional gives you access to the latest evidence-based treatments, providing you with the best possible chances for recovery. With the right support and resources, you'll be better equipped to overcome the effects of trauma, and move forward towards a brighter future.

II. Types of Professional Support for Trauma Recovery

When it comes to trauma recovery, seeking professional support is a critical step towards healing and finding peace. With the right resources and guidance, it's possible to overcome the effects of trauma and build a fulfilling, happy life.

In this section, we'll explore the different types of professional support available for those looking to recover from trauma.

Therapists and Counselors: Therapists and counselors are mental health professionals who specialize in helping individuals work through emotional and mental health challenges. They can provide support, guidance, and techniques to help individuals manage their symptoms and work towards recovery.

Psychologists and Psychiatrists: Psychologists and psychiatrists are mental health professionals who are trained to diagnose and treat mental health conditions, including trauma. They may use a

trauma. These groups provide a safe, supportive environment where individuals can share their experiences and connect with others who are also on a journey towards recovery.

Medication and Medical Treatments: For some individuals, medication and medical treatments may be necessary to manage the physical and emotional symptoms of trauma. This can include prescription medications to manage anxiety, depression, or sleep disorders, as well as medical treatments to address physical symptoms.

No matter what type of professional support you choose, it's important to find the right fit for you. With the right support and guidance, you can take the first steps towards healing and finding peace.

III. Finding the Right Professional Support for You

Recovering from trauma is a journey and finding the right professional support is a crucial step in that journey. Selecting a therapist or counselor can be an overwhelming experience, but it's essential to take the time to find someone who is the right fit for you. The goal is to work with a professional who can help you navigate the challenges of trauma recovery in a safe, supportive, and effective manner.

Considerations when selecting a therapist or counselor include:

Qualifications and credentials
Specializations in trauma recovery
Approach to therapy
Availability and location
It's important to understand the different approaches to therapy, such as Cognitive Behavioral Therapy, Eye Movement Desensitization and Reprocessing (EMDR), and Trauma-Focused Cognitive Behavioral Therapy, to determine which approach might be the best fit for you.

challenges of trauma recovery.

Finding the right professional support can be a challenging process, but the rewards are immense. With the right support, you can work through the effects of trauma and reclaim your life, so don't be afraid to take the first step towards healing.

Here are some questions that can help you find the right professional for you and build trust and rapport:

➢ What is your experience with treating individuals with similar traumatic experiences to mine?

➢ How do you approach therapy and what techniques do you use?

➢ Can you explain your philosophy on therapy and the role of the therapist?

➢ How do you measure progress and success in therapy?

➢ How do you handle sensitive or difficult topics that may arise during therapy?

➢ Are you licensed and insured, and do you have any certifications or specializations?

➢ What are your availability and scheduling policies, and how do you handle missed sessions?

➢ What are your fees and do you offer a sliding scale or insurance billing?

➢ Do you work collaboratively with other healthcare providers, such as a primary care physician or psychiatrist?

➢ Can you provide references or testimonials from previous clients?

Seeking professional support can be a big step, especially for those who have experienced trauma. There can be fear and shame associated with asking for help, but it's important to remember that this is a sign of strength, not weakness. By taking the first step towards recovery, you are making a choice to take control of your life and work towards a brighter future.

Making the decision to seek professional support can be challenging, but there are resources available to help you find a qualified therapist or counselor. You can start by speaking with your primary care doctor, reaching out to a mental health hotline, or searching online for local therapy or counseling services.

It's also important to consider the type of therapy or support that best suits your needs. Some people may benefit from individual therapy, while others may find group therapy to be more effective. It's okay to shop around and try a few different approaches until you find the right fit.

Once you've found a therapist or counselor, it's important to build trust and rapport with them. This can take time, but by working together and being open and honest about your experiences, you can build a strong therapeutic relationship that will support your recovery and growth.

Journal exercises that may help with overcoming fear and shame associated with seeking professional support:

Identifying fears: Write down all the fears that are holding you back from seeking help. This could include fear of judgement, fear of being vulnerable, fear of failure, etc.

Reframing fears: For each fear you identified, write down a reframed perspective. Try to find a positive or empowering angle for

Focus on these positives, rather than on the fears and shame that are holding you back.

Letter writing: Write a letter to yourself, or to a trusted friend or family member, expressing your fears and concerns about seeking help. Allow yourself to be vulnerable and honest in this letter, and remember that reaching out for help is a sign of strength, not weakness.

Mindfulness exercises: Practice mindfulness techniques, such as deep breathing, meditation, or progressive muscle relaxation, to calm your mind and body. This can help you to feel more in control, and less fearful and ashamed, as you take steps towards seeking professional support.

VII. Conclusion

Trauma recovery is a complex and challenging journey, but seeking professional support can be an essential step towards healing and improvement. Incorporating self-care and self-compassion practices into your daily routine can also be incredibly beneficial, and the two approaches complement each other nicely. Seeking professional support does not mean you are weak or that you have failed, but rather that you are making a conscious effort to prioritize your well-being and take control of your recovery. Whether you choose to work with a therapist, counselor, support group, or another professional, you will be taking a powerful step towards a brighter future. Remember that healing takes time and patience, but with the right support, you can and will get there. So, do not hesitate to reach out and take that first step today. You are worth it.

PART 4:
BUILDING A
SUPPORT SYSTEM

In the journey of trauma recovery, having a strong support system can be a crucial factor in promoting healing and growth. This section will explore various strategies for building a secure and supportive environment, including finding a safe place to stay, connecting with local resources and support groups, and creating a network of friends and family who can offer encouragement and care. Whether it's through reaching out to others or exploring available resources, this section will empower you to take steps towards constructing a supportive environment that can aid in your journey towards healing and recovery.

Finding a safe and secure place to call home can be a critical step in the healing journey after experiencing trauma. A safe living environment can help provide stability and a sense of security, allowing you to focus on your recovery and personal growth.

In this chapter, we will explore the different options for finding a safe place to stay and tips for making the transition as smooth as possible. Whether you are looking for temporary or long-term housing, there are resources and options available to help you find the right place for you.

I. Understanding the Importance of Safe Housing

The impact of trauma on your sense of safety and security
The role of stable housing in the recovery process
II. Options for Finding Safe Housing

Emergency shelters
Transitional housing
Affordable housing programs
Short-term rentals
III. Tips for Making the Transition to Safe Housing

Creating a budget and plan for your housing search
Navigating the housing application process
Finding support and resources to help with the transition
IV. Conclusion

The importance of prioritizing safe housing in your recovery journey
Encouragement to take the steps necessary to find a safe and secure place to call home.

I. Understanding the Importance of Safe Housing

added stress of worrying about their safety.

Having a safe place to stay is not just about having a roof over your head, but it's also about having a space where you feel secure, valued and respected. A place where you can relax, sleep soundly and simply be yourself without any fear of judgement or danger. A safe home environment is the foundation of recovery, providing individuals with the peace of mind they need to focus on the journey ahead.

It's essential to understand the impact that trauma has on our sense of safety and security, and the role that stable housing plays in our recovery. Without a safe and secure place to call home, it's difficult to feel grounded and focused, making it challenging to make progress in the healing process. By prioritizing the importance of safe housing, we can ensure that we have the foundation we need to begin the journey of healing and recovery.

Here is a checklist for the importance of safe housing in trauma recovery:

✓ Assessment of current living situation: Evaluate your current living situation and assess if it feels safe and secure to you.

✓ Identifying triggers: Identify any triggers that may impact your sense of safety and security within your current living environment.

✓ Researching housing options: Research and gather information on different housing options, such as shelters, transitional housing, or permanent housing.

✓ Creating a budget: Consider your financial situation and create a budget to help you determine what type of housing you can afford.

✓ Building a support network: Reach out to friends, family, or support groups for help and support in finding safe housing.

professional, such as a case manager, to assist you in finding safe housing.

✓ Making a decision: After researching and considering all options, make a decision on the type of housing that is best for you.

Remember, finding safe housing is an important step in your recovery process and should not be taken lightly. It is important to prioritize your safety and well-being, and seek the help of others if needed.

II. Options for Finding Safe Housing

When it comes to finding a safe place to stay, there are several options available to those in need. It's important to consider your unique situation and what kind of support you need when making a decision. Here are some of the options to consider:

Emergency Shelters: If you are in immediate danger and need a place to stay right away, an emergency shelter may be your best option. These shelters offer a safe and secure environment, as well as basic necessities like food, clothing, and shelter.

Transitional Housing: Transitional housing programs offer a stepping stone between emergency shelters and permanent housing. They often provide longer-term stays, as well as support services like job training, financial planning, and counseling.

Affordable Housing Programs: Affordable housing programs are designed to provide safe and affordable homes for those in need. These programs can vary greatly in their offerings, so it's important to research the options available to you and determine what will best fit your needs.

specific needs, budget, and overall goals for recovery. With a little research and some planning, you can find a safe and secure place to stay that will support your healing and well-being.

In conclusion, finding a safe place to stay is a critical aspect of trauma recovery. Safe housing provides a foundation of stability and security, allowing individuals to focus on their mental, emotional, and physical well-being. While the search for safe housing can be challenging, it is important to prioritize this aspect of recovery. There are several options available, including emergency shelters, transitional housing, affordable housing programs, and short-term rentals. It is important to take the necessary steps to find a safe and secure place to call home. Remember that your health and well-being are worth investing in, and seeking a safe place to stay is an important step in your recovery journey.

Additional exercises for this chapter:

Write a list of the things you associate with feeling safe and secure, then reflect on what specific elements are important to you in your home environment

_____

_____

_____

_____

_____

Imagine your ideal safe space, and draw or create a visual representation of it

_____

_____

_____

Make a list of all the resources available to you in your community and research each one to learn more about the options they offer

_____

_____

_____

_____

_____

Take a virtual tour of different types of housing options, such as emergency shelters or short-term rentals, to get a better understanding of what's available

_____

_____

_____

_____

_____

Reflect on the steps you've taken to prioritize your housing needs, and make a list of things you can do to maintain a safe and secure living environment

Write a letter to yourself in the future, detailing the steps you took to find safe housing and the impact it has had on your healing journey.

Example:

Dear Future Self,

I hope this letter finds you well and in a safe and comfortable home. As I write this, I am in the process of finding a safe and suitable

[Insert details of the steps you took to find safe housing, including any challenges you faced and how you overcame them.]

I am proud of myself for persevering through the obstacles and for not giving up on finding a place where I can feel secure and at peace. Finding safe housing has been a crucial step in my healing journey, and I am confident that it will continue to have a positive impact on my well-being for years to come.

[Insert details about the impact finding safe housing has had on your healing journey, including any changes you have noticed in your mental and emotional state, relationships, and overall quality of life.]

I am grateful for this experience and the lessons it has taught me. I hope that, in reading this letter, you are reminded of the strength and resilience you possess and the importance of taking care of yourself and your needs.

With love and gratitude,

[Your Name]

I. Introduction to Local Resources and Support Groups

Explanation of what local resources and support groups are
Importance of connecting with these resources during the recovery journey

II. Identifying Local Resources and Support Groups

How to find local resources and support groups in your community
Benefits of using online resources and directories

III. The Benefits of Connecting with Local Resources and Support Groups

Improved access to mental health services
Increased sense of community and belonging
Opportunities for peer support and connection

IV. Engaging with Local Resources and Support Groups

Tips for making the most of your involvement
Overcoming barriers to participation
How to find the right group for you

V. Conclusion

Emphasis on the importance of connecting with local resources and support groups
Encouragement to take the steps necessary to find the support you need.

go through it alone. In this chapter, we will look at how connecting with others who have gone through similar experiences can be a powerful tool in healing and growth. We will also discuss how connecting with local resources can provide practical support and resources to help you feel empowered and in control of your recovery. So let's dive into how you can start building your support network today.

II. Identifying Local Resources and Support Groups

Connecting with local resources and support groups can be a valuable part of your trauma recovery journey. In this section, we will explore how to find these resources and the benefits of using them.

One of the best ways to find local resources and support groups is through online directories and resources. Many communities have websites and databases that list support groups and resources, along with contact information and descriptions of the services they offer. This can be a great starting point for your search.

In addition to online resources, there are a number of other ways to find local support groups and resources. You can start by reaching out to your doctor, therapist, or other healthcare provider for recommendations. You may also be able to find support groups through local organizations, such as religious organizations, schools, or community centers.

Using local resources and support groups can provide a wealth of benefits for your recovery journey. These resources can help you connect with others who have experienced similar traumas, and can provide you with the support and encouragement you need to keep moving forward. They can also be a source of information and guidance, helping you navigate the complex landscape of trauma recovery.

III. The Benefits of Connecting with Local Resources and Support Groups

When it comes to recovering from trauma, it's important to have a support system in place. This can include professional therapists and counselors, as well as friends, family, and community resources. In this section, we'll explore the benefits of connecting with local resources and support groups, and how they can help you on your journey to recovery.

Improved access to mental health services - Local resources and support groups can provide you with a wealth of information about mental health services in your area, including therapists, support groups, and medical treatments. This can be especially helpful for individuals who are struggling to access these services on their own.

Increased sense of community and belonging - Connecting with others who have experienced similar traumas can be incredibly healing. You'll feel like you're not alone, and you'll be surrounded by individuals who understand what you're going through. This can lead to a stronger sense of community and belonging, which is crucial for building resilience and maintaining positive mental health.

Opportunities for peer support and connection - Joining a support group or connecting with local resources can provide you with a space to share your story and receive support from others who have been in your shoes. You can benefit from the wisdom and experiences of others, and learn coping skills and strategies that have worked for others in your community. This kind of peer support can be incredibly valuable and help you feel more connected and empowered as you navigate your journey to recovery.

they also help you feel more connected and a part of a community. But how do you make the most of your involvement in these groups? Here are some tips to help you get started:

Be proactive: Don't wait for someone else to reach out to you. Take the initiative and make the first move. Attend meetings, events, or workshops that interest you, and introduce yourself to others.

Be open-minded: Be open to different approaches and perspectives. Even if something doesn't resonate with you at first, keep an open mind and give it a try. You never know what you might learn or gain from others.

Ask for help: If you're feeling overwhelmed or unsure about how to participate, reach out to the leaders or organizers of the group and ask for guidance. They will likely be more than happy to help.

Overcome barriers: If you're facing barriers that are preventing you from participating in local resources and support groups, find ways to overcome them. This might mean seeking financial assistance, transportation, or childcare.

Find the right group for you: Not all local resources and support groups are created equal. It's important to find a group that aligns with your values, beliefs, and needs. Take the time to research different groups and attend a few meetings before making a decision.

By following these tips, you'll be well on your way to making the most of your involvement in local resources and support groups, and taking an important step in your trauma recovery journey.

Conclusion

As you embark on your journey towards recovery from trauma, connecting with local resources and support groups can play a critical role in helping you heal and rebuild your life. Whether it's through the time to take the steps necessary to find the support you need. Whether it's reaching out to local organizations, connecting with peer groups, or seeking out online resources, there are a variety of ways to get involved and engage with the support available to you.

Remember, healing and recovery is a journey that requires time, effort, and a willingness to be vulnerable. But with the right support and resources in place, you can overcome the barriers that stand in your way and build a brighter, more fulfilling future for yourself. So take the first step today, and start connecting with the support you need to thrive.

'

FRIENDS AND FAMILY

I. Understanding the Importance of a Supportive Network
A. The impact of trauma on relationships
B. The role of social support in the recovery process

II. Building and Maintaining Relationships with Friends and Family
A. Repairing damaged relationships
B. Strategies for developing new, supportive relationships
C. Navigating boundaries and maintaining healthy relationships

III. Finding Support Beyond Friends and Family
A. Building a network of supportive peers
B. Building relationships with allies and advocates
C. Navigating relationships with acquaintances and strangers

IV. Conclusion
A. Emphasis on the importance of building a supportive network
B. Encouragement to take the steps necessary to build and maintain supportive relationships.

benefits of having a supportive network and how to build one from the ground up. Whether it is through strengthening existing relationships or making new connections, we will cover the steps you can take to create a network of support and comfort. So, let's get started on this important aspect of your recovery journey.

I. Understanding the Importance of a Supportive Network
A. The impact of trauma on relationships
Trauma can have a profound impact on our relationships with others, leading to feelings of isolation, mistrust, and difficulty connecting with those around us. In order to recover and heal from trauma, it is important to understand the role that supportive relationships play in our lives.

B. The role of social support in the recovery process
Research has shown that having a strong network of supportive friends and family members is essential for long-term mental health and well-being. This support can help us to feel less alone, to work through difficult emotions, and to cope with the challenges of recovery. Whether through shared experiences, emotional connection, or practical assistance, supportive relationships can play a key role in helping us to heal and rebuild after trauma.

Here are a few journal exercises to help build understanding of the importance of a supportive network in the context of trauma recovery:

Reflect on your current relationships: Take some time to reflect on the people in your life and how they've impacted your recovery journey. Write down any thoughts, feelings, or insights that come to mind.

Explore the impact of trauma on relationships: Consider how trauma has affected your relationships with friends, family, and loved ones. Write about any challenges you've faced and how these relationships have helped or hindered your recovery.

Practice gratitude: Write a letter to someone in your life who has been a source of support and gratitude. Express how they've helped you and why their presence is so valuable in your life.

II. Building and Maintaining Relationships with Friends and Family

Building and Maintaining Relationships with Friends and Family

Trauma can have a significant impact on our relationships with those around us, making it difficult to feel connected and supported by the people who matter most. However, developing and maintaining healthy relationships with friends and family can play a crucial role in the recovery process. In this section, we will explore strategies for repairing damaged relationships, building new, supportive relationships, and navigating boundaries to maintain healthy connections.

A. Repairing Damaged Relationships

Reflect on the relationships that have been impacted by your trauma.

_____

_____

_____

_____

_____

Consider what needs to be addressed in order to repair these relationships.

_____

_____

Write a letter to the person you would like to repair the relationship with, expressing your feelings and what you hope to achieve. You may choose to deliver this letter or simply keep it as a reminder of your intentions.

_____

_____

_____

_____

_____

When ready, reach out to the person and express your willingness to work towards healing the relationship.

_____

_____

_____

_____

_____

Practice active listening, open communication, and be patient as the process of repairing a damaged relationship can take time.

Trauma can cause strain on even the closest relationships. If you have experienced trauma, it may be necessary to work on repairing relationships with friends and family that have been affected. Here are some tips for repairing damaged relationships:

Acknowledge what has happened - If a relationship has been impacted by trauma, it is important to acknowledge the situation and how it has affected both parties.

Express your feelings - Share how you feel about the situation and the relationship, and listen to the other person's perspective.

a therapist to support the process of repairing relationships.

Strategies for Developing New, Supportive Relationships

In addition to repairing damaged relationships, it is important to build new, supportive relationships to help you on your recovery journey. Here are some tips for developing new relationships:

Seek out social opportunities - Joining clubs, groups, or classes that align with your interests can help you meet new people and form connections.

Volunteer - Volunteering for a cause you believe in can provide a sense of purpose and help you build relationships with like-minded individuals.

Be open and honest - When forming new relationships, be open and honest about your experiences, including your history of trauma, to build trust and understanding.

B. Strategies for Developing New, Supportive Relationships

Consider what qualities you are looking for in a supportive relationship.

_____

_____

_____

_____

_____

Identify opportunities to meet new people and form new relationships, such as joining a club, volunteering, or taking a class.

_____

_____

Be open and authentic about your needs and experiences.

Practice good communication and active listening skills in your new relationships.

Seek out people who share similar interests and values to build strong and supportive relationships.

In addition to repairing damaged relationships, it is important to build new, supportive relationships to help you on your recovery journey. Here are some tips for developing new relationships:

Seek out social opportunities - Joining clubs, groups, or classes that align with your interests can help you meet new people and form connections.

Volunteer - Volunteering for a cause you believe in can provide a sense of purpose and help you build relationships with like-minded individuals.

Be open and honest - When forming new relationships, be open and honest about your experiences, including your history of trauma, to build trust and understanding.

C. Navigating Boundaries and Maintaining Healthy Relationships

Identify your personal boundaries and what is important to you in a relationship.

Communicate your boundaries to others and respect the boundaries of others.

Be aware of signs of unhealthy relationships, such as feeling constantly drained or disrespected.

Practice self-care and seek support when needed to maintain healthy relationships.

Celebrate and acknowledge the positive aspects of your relationships and take time to address any challenges in a healthy and constructive manner.

Once you have repaired damaged relationships and formed new, supportive relationships, it is important to maintain healthy connections.

key to maintaining

healthy relationships. Share your thoughts, feelings, and concerns in a respectful and open manner.

Set and respect boundaries - Make sure that both you and the other person understand each other's boundaries, and respect them moving forward.

Prioritize self-care - Maintaining healthy relationships requires a focus on self-care. Prioritize your own well-being, and communicate with those around you to ensure that your needs are being met.

In conclusion, repairing damaged relationships, developing new, supportive relationships, and maintaining healthy relationships are all important steps in the recovery journey. By following these tips and strategies, you can build and maintain a supportive network of friends and family that will help you on your journey to healing and recovery.

Exercises

Here are a few exercises related to the topic of building and maintaining relationships with friends and family in the context of trauma recovery:

Reflecting on Damaged Relationships: Write down a list of relationships that have been impacted by your trauma experience. Reflect on what you would like to repair or improve in each of these relationships.

_____

_____

_____

_____

_____

Example:

Dear [Name of Person],

I hope this message finds you well. I would like to have a conversation with you about our relationship. I have been thinking about our interactions lately and have realized that there are areas where I could improve our communication.

I would like to focus on using mindful communication techniques during our conversation, such as active listening, avoiding judgment, and speaking authentically. Active listening means truly paying attention to what you are saying and trying to understand your perspective. Avoiding judgment means not making assumptions or thinking of preconceived notions, but instead trying to understand where you are coming from. Speaking authentically means being honest and true to myself, while also being respectful and considerate of your feelings.

Can we schedule a time to have this conversation in person or via phone/video call? I believe that by using mindful communication techniques, we can repair or improve our relationship and move forward in a positive direction.

Thank you for taking the time to read this message, and I look forward to speaking with you soon.

Best regards,

[Your Name]

Developing New Relationships: Write down a list of activities, hobbies, or community events that interest you. Plan to attend one of these events or activities, and focus on making connections with new people who share similar interests.

Boundary-Setting: Write down a list of situations that make you feel uncomfortable or violated in your relationships. Practice setting healthy boundaries by clearly communicating your needs and expectations to your friends and family.

Allies and Advocates: Think about people in your life who you consider allies or advocates. Write down what makes them supportive and what you appreciate about their role in your life. Try to cultivate more relationships with individuals who have similar qualities.

Building a Supportive Network: Write down a list of friends, family members, and other individuals who you consider to be part of your support network. Reflect on what makes each person supportive, and how you can maintain and strengthen your relationships with them.

_____

_____

_____

_____

_____

Navigating Relationships with Acquaintances and Strangers: Practice building relationships with acquaintances and strangers by taking small steps to engage in conversations, ask questions, and share your interests. Reflect on what you can learn from these relationships and how they can add value to your life.

_____

_____

_____

_____

healing and recovery journey. The impact of trauma can often leave us feeling isolated and disconnected, but by reaching out and building meaningful relationships with others, we can regain a sense of community and belonging.

Building a network of supportive friends and family, repairing damaged relationships, and developing new relationships takes time and effort. However, the rewards are immeasurable and can have a profound impact on our lives. By prioritizing our relationships and investing in them, we can create a foundation of support that will see us through even the toughest times.

So don't be afraid to take action and start building your network of support today. Whether it's reaching out to old friends, joining a local support group, or simply opening yourself up to new connections, taking these steps can make a huge difference in your healing and recovery process. Remember, you are not alone, and with the right support, you can overcome anything.

PART 5
NAVIGATING THE
LEGAL SYSTEM

In the aftermath of trauma, navigating the legal system can feel overwhelming and intimidating. However, it's important to understand your rights and options for legal protection. This section of the guide will provide information and support for working with law enforcement and the court system, as well as preparing for trial and giving testimony. Whether you're seeking justice for a crime committed against you, or trying to rebuild your life after a traumatic experience, this section is here to help. From understanding your rights, to getting the support you need, we'll guide you through the complex process of navigating the legal system. Let's get started.

I. Overview of Legal Protection for Victims of Stalking and Abuse
A. Overview of Stalking
1. Real-life stalking
2. Cyber stalking
B. The impact of false allegations
C. Military personnel and the legal system

II. Understanding Your Legal Rights
A. Overview of legal rights for victims of abuse
B. Understanding the restraining order process
C. Preparing for a restraining order hearing

III. Options for Legal Protection
A. Filing a police report
B. Obtaining a restraining order
C. Seeking a restraining order against military personnel
D. Seeking a restraining order against former military personnel

IV. Navigating the Legal System
A. Working with law enforcement
B. Understanding the court system
C. Preparing for trial
D. Giving testimony in court

V. Conclusion
A. Emphasis on the importance of understanding your legal rights and options
B. Encouragement to take the steps necessary to protect yourself legally.

emails, and engaging in surveillance.

Real-life Stalking

Real-life stalking refers to a pattern of behavior in which one person repeatedly harasses or threatens another person, causing them to feel fear for their safety. This type of stalking can take many forms, including:

Following someone: This can involve physically following the victim, such as by car, on foot, or through public transportation. The stalker may also use technology to monitor the victim's movements, such as through GPS tracking or by using social media to keep tabs on their location.

Making threatening phone calls or emails: The stalker may use phone calls, emails, text messages, or other forms of communication to harass or threaten the victim. This can include making repeated calls, sending threatening messages, or leaving harassing voicemails.

Engaging in surveillance: The stalker may use various methods to monitor the victim's movements and activities, such as watching their home or workplace, accessing their personal information, or using technology to track their location.

These behaviors can cause the victim to feel scared, helpless, and trapped, and can have a significant impact on their mental health and well-being. Stalking is a serious crime, and it is important for victims to understand their rights and options for legal protection.

B. The impact of false allegations

In some cases, the abuser or abuser may try to turn the tables and make false allegations against the victim, alleging that they are the ones who are being stalked or harassed. This can create confusion and complicate the legal process, as the victim may need to defend themselves against these false accusations.

challenges and complexities. Military personnel may face different rules and procedures when it comes to filing a report, pursuing legal action, or seeking protection from stalking or abuse. It is important for military personnel to understand their rights and options for legal protection, and to work with military support organizations and legal advocates who are familiar with the specific challenges they face.

II. Protecting Yourself from Real-life Stalking

If you are a victim of real-life stalking, it is important to take steps to protect yourself and to seek legal help. This may include:

Documenting the stalking: Keep a record of all instances of stalking, including dates, times, and details of the incidents. This can be helpful in building a case for legal action.

Telling others: Let friends, family, and coworkers know what is happening, and ask for their support. This can help create a network of people who can help you stay safe and feel supported.

Seeking legal help: Work with a local domestic violence or victim services organization, or reach out to law enforcement for help. An attorney can help you understand your rights and options for legal protection, and can assist you in filing a report, obtaining a restraining order, or pursuing legal action.

Staying safe: Take steps to stay safe, such as changing your routine, avoiding the stalker, and using technology to help you stay connected with friends and family.

By understanding your rights and options for legal protection, and taking steps to protect yourself from real-life stalking, you can reclaim your sense of safety and control.

2. Cyber stalking
B. The impact of false allegations

harassment, cyber bullying, and the use of spyware or other software to monitor someone's activity.

While cyber stalking can be particularly damaging to its victims, it can also be difficult to detect and prosecute. Victims of cyber stalking may feel helpless and alone, and may struggle to find effective ways to protect themselves.

One of the biggest challenges in addressing cyber stalking is the potential for false allegations. In some cases, someone may make false accusations of cyber stalking in order to manipulate or harm another person. This can be especially problematic in the legal system, where false allegations can cloud the truth and make it difficult for victims to receive the protection they need.

It is important for individuals who are being stalked to understand their rights and options for legal protection. This includes seeking help from law enforcement and the court system, as well as taking steps to protect themselves from further harm. By working together with local resources and support groups, victims of cyber stalking can take the steps necessary to find safety and security in the face of this growing threat.

Military personnel and the legal system

The legal system can be complicated and overwhelming, especially for military personnel who may have unique challenges and considerations. When dealing with stalking and abuse, it is important to understand your rights and options for legal protection.

One of the main differences for military personnel is the jurisdiction and venue for their cases. Military members can face legal proceedings in both civilian and military courts, and the appropriate venue will depend on the specific circumstances of the case.

Additionally, the military has its own set of laws and regulations, such as the Uniform Code of Military Justice (UCMJ), which governs the conduct of military personnel. The UCMJ provides specific protections for victims of domestic violence and stalking, and military personnel who have been accused of abuse may face disciplinary action under the UCMJ in addition to any civilian charges.

It is important for military personnel to understand their rights and options under the UCMJ and to work with a knowledgeable attorney who has experience in both military and civilian legal proceedings.

In addition it is important for military personnel to be aware of the resources available to them, such as the Victims' Legal Counsel (VLC) program, which provides free legal representation to eligible military victims of crime.

When the abuser is a former military personnel and the spouse is not affiliated with the military, the legal process may be slightly different. However, there are still several options for seeking protection and support.

One option is to seek a restraining order through the civilian court system. In some cases, a civilian court may have jurisdiction over a former military member if the abuse took place off-base. The process for obtaining a restraining order is similar to that of any other civilian case.

Another option is to seek assistance from the Department of Veterans Affairs (VA). The VA provides resources and support for military veterans and their families, including those who have experienced domestic violence or abuse. The VA can provide counseling services, as well as assistance in obtaining restraining orders and other forms of legal protection.

It is also important to reach out to local domestic violence organizations or hotlines for support and resources. They may be able and support available to help you stay safe and protect your rights.

In conclusion, understanding your rights and options for legal protection is crucial for military personnel who have been victims of stalking and abuse. By working with an experienced attorney and utilizing available resources, military personnel can navigate the legal system and pursue justice for themselves and their families.

II. Understanding Your Legal Rights: the full break down

A. Overview of Legal Rights for Victims of Abuse

As a victim of abuse, it is important to understand your legal rights. The laws surrounding domestic abuse and stalking vary by state, but there are general legal protections in place for victims of abuse. These include the right to seek a restraining order, file a police report, and pursue criminal charges against the abuser. Additionally, you have the right to receive support and protection from law enforcement and the court system.

For example, in many states, if a victim of domestic abuse seeks a restraining order, the abuser is legally prohibited from coming within a certain distance of the victim and from having any form of contact with the victim. In some cases, a restraining order may also require the abuser to surrender firearms. If the abuser violates the restraining order, they can face criminal charges.

In addition, victims of abuse have the right to file a police report and to pursue criminal charges against their abuser. This can result in the abuser being arrested and facing criminal consequences, such as imprisonment and fines.

It is important to note that these legal protections are in place to ensure that victims of abuse are safe and that perpetrators are held accountable for their actions. If you are a victim of abuse, it is important to take advantage of the legal protections available to you

A restraining order is a legal order issued by a judge that requires an individual to stop harassing, threatening, or injuring another person. There are two main types of restraining orders: temporary and permanent. A temporary restraining order can be obtained quickly, often without the abuser present, and is typically in place for a few weeks. A permanent restraining order, on the other hand, requires a hearing and may be in place for several years.

In order to obtain a restraining order, you will need to file a request with your local court. You will also need to provide evidence of the abuse, such as police reports, witness statements, and any other documentation that supports your case. Once the restraining order is granted, it is important to follow the terms of the order and to report any violations to the police immediately.

C. Preparing for a Restraining Order Hearing

If you are seeking a permanent restraining order, you will need to attend a hearing in front of a judge. This can be a nerve-wracking experience, but it is important to be prepared. You should gather all of the evidence you have related to the abuse, including police reports, witness statements, and any other documentation. You should also prepare a statement explaining why you are seeking the restraining order and what you hope to achieve by doing so.

It is also helpful to have a support system in place, such as friends or family members, who can accompany you to the hearing. Having someone there to provide moral support can make a big difference in helping you feel more confident and prepared.

Remember, seeking a restraining order is a serious step and should not be taken lightly. However, it can also be a powerful tool for protecting yourself and ensuring your safety. By understanding your legal rights and preparing for a restraining order hearing, you can feel more confident and empowered as you navigate the legal system.

be a daunting task. However, it is important to understand that there are many resources available to help you through the process. In this chapter, we will explore the steps you can take to work with law enforcement, understand the court system, prepare for trial, and give testimony in court.

I. Working with Law Enforcement

As a victim of abuse or stalking, it is important to seek the protection of law enforcement. When you report the abuse or stalking, law enforcement agencies are trained to respond and provide you with the necessary resources to help you through the legal process. Reporting the abuse is a crucial step in seeking legal protection and can help in obtaining a restraining order, arresting the abuser, and building a case against them.

Working with law enforcement can be a daunting experience, but it is important to remember that they are there to help you. They have the training, experience, and resources to provide you with support and assistance throughout the process. When you make a report, law enforcement will take a statement from you and gather any evidence that may be relevant to the case. They will also inform you of your rights and help you navigate the legal process.

In some cases, law enforcement may be able to make an arrest on the spot. However, in other cases, they may need to gather additional evidence before making an arrest. Either way, it is important to provide law enforcement with as much information as possible about the abuse or stalking you have experienced. This will help them to build a stronger case against the offender and increase the chances of a successful outcome.

If you are in immediate danger, do not hesitate to call 911. Law enforcement is equipped to handle emergencies and will respond promptly to your call. If you are not in immediate danger, you can make a report to your local police department. You can also contact a domestic violence or stalking hotline for additional support and resources.

as much information as possible about the abuse or stalking you have experienced to increase the chances of a successful outcome.

II. Understanding the Court System

In a restraining order hearing, a judge will determine if a restraining order should be granted to protect you from the abuser. This can include prohibiting the abuser from contacting you, entering your home, or having any contact with you. The court process can be lengthy and stressful, but it is important to understand how it works so you can be prepared and take an active role in your case.

Before the hearing, you may want to seek the advice of an attorney or a victim advocate to help you understand your rights and options. During the hearing, the judge will hear evidence and testimony from both sides and make a decision based on the law and the facts presented. It is important to be prepared to present your case in a clear and concise manner, and to have any evidence or witnesses ready to support your claims.

The court system can be a complicated and challenging process, but it is an important part of seeking legal protection. By understanding how the court system works, you can be better prepared to navigate it and protect yourself from abuse and stalking.

III. Preparing for Trial

In the court of law, preparation is key to success. If your case goes to trial, it is crucial to be as prepared as possible. This will ensure that you are able to present your case in the best light possible and increase the chances of obtaining the legal protection you seek.

To prepare for trial, you must gather all of the evidence that supports your case. This may include photos, emails, text messages, or any other form of documentation that will support your claims. You should also locate and interview any witnesses who may have seen or includes understanding the charges against you, the potential outcomes of the case, and the options available to you for seeking legal protection.

Seeking the assistance of an attorney who specializes in domestic abuse and stalking cases can be extremely beneficial in preparing for trial. An experienced attorney can help you navigate the legal system, advise you on the best course of action, and provide you with the support and guidance you need to be successful.

In the words of Dale Carnegie, "Success is getting what you want. Happiness is wanting what you get." By preparing thoroughly for your trial, you are increasing your chances of success and obtaining the legal protection you seek. Remember, being prepared is the key to unlocking your full potential and reaching your goals.

IV. Giving Testimony in Court

As a victim of abuse or stalking, giving testimony in court can seem like a daunting task. However, it is important to remember that your testimony is critical in helping to bring justice to the situation. In this chapter, we will explore tips and strategies for giving effective testimony in court, so that you can approach this important moment with confidence.

First and foremost, it is essential to be truthful and clear in your testimony. The judge and jury want to hear the facts of the case, and it is your responsibility to provide them with accurate and detailed information. Be prepared to answer questions about what happened, when it happened, and who was involved.

It may be helpful to practice giving your testimony before the trial, so that you are comfortable with what you will be asked in court. You can do this with a trusted friend or family member, or with an attorney who specializes in domestic abuse and stalking cases.

Finally, it is essential to approach your testimony with confidence and a positive attitude. Remember that you are not alone and that you are doing a valuable service by speaking out against abuse and stalking. By giving your testimony in a clear and confident manner, you can help bring an end to the abuse and help to protect others from similar experiences in the future.

In conclusion, giving testimony in court is a crucial part of the legal process for victims of abuse and stalking. Although it can be a daunting experience, approaching the situation with confidence and preparedness can make a significant impact in achieving justice. By staying truthful and clear in your testimony, you are taking a bold step towards bringing an end to the abuse and stalking and towards a brighter, safer future. Remember, your testimony has the power to make a difference and bring peace of mind to yourself and others who have been affected by these crimes. So have faith in yourself, stay focused, and know that you are doing the right thing.

PART VI.
REBUILDING YOUR LIFE

A. Explanation of the importance of rebuilding after abuse or stalking

B. Overview of the steps involved in rebuilding

II. Dealing with Financial Stress

A. Understanding the financial impact of abuse or stalking

B. Creating a budget and managing finances

C. Finding resources for financial assistance

III. Finding a Job and Stable Source of Income

A. Understanding the importance of work in rebuilding your life

B. Strategies for finding a job and building a career

C. Building a stable financial foundation

IV. Building Self-Esteem and a Positive Self-Image

A. Understanding the impact of abuse and stalking on self-esteem

B. Strategies for building self-esteem and confidence

C. Creating a positive self-image and self-identity

V. Conclusion

A. Summary of the steps involved in rebuilding after abuse or stalking

B. Encouragement to focus on personal growth and a positive future

C. Final thoughts and resources for support.

In the aftermath of abuse and stalking, it can be difficult to pick up the pieces and move forward. However, with the right support and resources, it is possible to rebuild your life and create a brighter future. This section will focus on dealing with financial stress, finding employment, and building self-esteem as key steps towards recovery and empowerment. In the words of Brené Brown, "Courage starts with showing up and letting ourselves be seen." By taking these steps towards a better life, you are demonstrating your strength, resilience, and determination to create a better future for yourself.

involved in doing so. Whether you are just starting your journey or are well on your way, it is important to approach the process with an open mind and a commitment to your own well-being. With the right support and resources, you can create a brighter future and live a life that is full of hope and joy.

Explanation of the importance of rebuilding after abuse or stalking

As a survivor of abuse or stalking, the journey towards healing and recovery can be a long and challenging one. However, it is important to remember that rebuilding your life is a crucial step in the healing process. By taking control of your situation and reclaiming your power, you can create a new future filled with hope and resilience. In this chapter, we will explore the importance of rebuilding your life after experiencing abuse or stalking.

When we experience trauma, it can be easy to feel like our lives are spiraling out of control. We may struggle with feelings of fear, anxiety, and shame, and feel like there is no way to regain our sense of safety and security. However, it is important to understand that rebuilding your life after abuse or stalking is not just about fixing the damage that has been done – it is also about reclaiming your power and finding a sense of purpose in the aftermath of trauma.

By focusing on rebuilding your life, you can begin to heal from the wounds of your experience and start to create a future that is truly yours. Whether you are working on your financial stability, finding a job, or building self-esteem, the process of rebuilding can be empowering and help you to reclaim your sense of agency and control.

So if you are a survivor of abuse or stalking, know that you are not alone and that there is hope for a brighter future. With the right tools and support, you can begin the journey towards rebuilding your life and creating a new path filled with strength, resilience, and hope.

control over your life, build self-esteem, and create a positive future. In this chapter, we will provide an overview of the steps involved in rebuilding, including dealing with financial stress, finding a job, and building self-esteem.

The process of rebuilding requires courage and vulnerability, but it can also be incredibly empowering. By taking control of your life and focusing on your own well-being, you can begin to heal from the trauma of abuse and stalking and create a brighter future for yourself. With time and support, you will find that you are stronger than you ever thought possible and capable of overcoming any obstacle.

II. Dealing with Financial Stress

Dealing with financial stress can be a challenging aspect of rebuilding your life after abuse or stalking. However, it is important to take control of your finances in order to create stability and security. This involves creating a budget, finding ways to reduce expenses, and finding ways to increase your income. Brené Brown's research on vulnerability and shame highlights the importance of taking action, even when it feels uncomfortable or scary, in order to build resilience and overcome obstacles. By taking control of your finances, you can reclaim your power and set yourself on a path towards financial stability and security.

Understanding the financial impact of abuse or stalking

The impact of abuse or stalking can extend far beyond just the physical and emotional toll. Unfortunately, it can also have a significant financial impact, leaving victims struggling to make ends meet and provide for themselves and their families. In this chapter, we'll explore the various ways that abuse and stalking can impact finances and what steps you can take to get back on track.

First, it's important to understand that abuse and stalking can lead to lost wages. Whether it's because you have to miss work to attend

In addition to lost wages, abuse and stalking can also lead to unexpected expenses. This might include the cost of moving to a safer location, paying for a restraining order or legal fees, or covering the cost of medical bills. All of these unexpected expenses can add up quickly, leaving you with even more financial stress.

The good news is that there are steps you can take to regain control of your finances. This might include seeking the assistance of a financial advisor, creating a budget, and taking steps to increase your income. Additionally, there are resources available to help you, such as victim compensation programs, financial assistance programs, and support groups.

It's important to remember that rebuilding your finances will take time, but with a clear plan and the right resources, it is possible. By taking steps to manage your finances and improve your financial stability, you'll be able to focus on your healing and rebuilding your life after abuse or stalking.

B. Creating a budget and managing finances

In the aftermath of abuse or stalking, it can be difficult to navigate the financial stress that often comes with the situation. But it's important to remember that you have the power to take control of your finances and create stability in your life. One of the first steps in doing this is to create a budget.

Creating a budget may seem daunting, but it's a simple and effective tool for managing your finances. It allows you to see exactly where your money is going and make informed decisions about how to allocate your resources. The key to creating a successful budget is to be realistic and consistent.

Start by tracking your spending for a few weeks to get a clear picture of your financial situation. Make a list of all your income and

Once you have a clear understanding of your finances, you can begin to create your budget. Set realistic goals for your spending and stick to them. It may be helpful to automate your savings so that you're putting money away each month without even thinking about it. And remember, it's okay to adjust your budget as your situation changes. The important thing is to have a plan and stick to it.

Taking control of your finances is an empowering step towards rebuilding your life after abuse or stalking. With a budget in place, you can focus on the other aspects of your life and continue to move forward with confidence and resilience.

Exercises

There are a number of exercises that can help you create a budget and manage your finances, including the following:

Tracking your expenses: Keeping track of all your expenses, both large and small, can help you see where your money is going and identify areas where you can cut back.

Making a list of monthly expenses: Make a list of all your monthly expenses, including rent or mortgage payments, utility bills, transportation costs, and food and entertainment expenses.

Prioritizing expenses: Once you have a list of all your expenses, prioritize them based on their importance. For example, you may consider necessities like rent, utilities, and food as more important than entertainment expenses.

Allocating a budget for each category: Once you have prioritized your expenses, allocate a budget for each category. Be sure to include a cushion for unexpected expenses.

Reviewing and adjusting your budget: Review your budget regularly and adjust it as needed to ensure you are on track to meet your financial goals.

truly necessary.

Seeking support: Finally, don't hesitate to seek support from friends, family, or a financial advisor if you need help creating a budget and managing your finances.

SOURCE OF INCOME

I. Introduction to Finding a Job
A. Explanation of the importance of financial stability after abuse or stalking
B. Overview of the steps involved in finding a job

II. Assessing Your Skills and Interests
A. Understanding your strengths and abilities
B. Identifying job opportunities that align with your skills and interests

III. Creating a Job Search Plan
A. Setting goals and objectives for your job search
B. Developing a strategy for finding job opportunities
C. Networking and building connections with potential employers

IV. Applying for Jobs and Preparing for Interviews
A. Writing a strong resume and cover letter
B. Researching potential employers and preparing for interviews
C. Tips for making a positive impression during an interview

V. Building a Stable Source of Income
A. Understanding the importance of consistent income
B. Tips for budgeting and saving money
C. Exploring opportunities for additional income streams

VI. Conclusion
A. Summary of key takeaways from the chapter
B. Emphasizing the importance of perseverance and persistence in finding a job and building a stable source of income.

It is an incredibly challenging and difficult task to pick up the pieces after experiencing abuse or stalking. Rebuilding your life requires a great deal of courage, resilience, and determination. One important aspect of this rebuilding process is finding a job and creating a stable source of income. This may seem daunting, especially given the financial impact of abuse or stalking, but I want you to know that it is possible to start a new chapter and create the life you deserve.

In this chapter, we will explore the different strategies and tools you can use to find a job and build a stable financial future. We will also talk about the importance of self-care and self-compassion as you navigate this process. Remember, you are not alone and you are capable of creating a bright future for yourself.

A. Explanation of the Importance of Financial Stability after Abuse or Stalking

Financial stability is an important aspect of the rebuilding process after experiencing abuse or stalking. Having a stable source of income can help you to regain control over your life and take the necessary steps to move forward. It can also help to alleviate financial stress and provide you with the resources you need to feel safe and secure.

B. Overview of the Steps Involved in Finding a Job

Finding a job can seem overwhelming, especially if you've been out of the workforce for a while. But with the right resources and support, you can find a job that fits your skills and interests and provides you with financial stability. This chapter will guide you through the steps involved in finding a job and creating a stable source of income.

II. Assessing Your Skills and Interests

In the aftermath of abuse or stalking, it can be difficult to think about the future and rebuilding your life. However, one of the key steps to creating a stable source of income is to assess your skills and

A. Understanding Your Strengths and Abilities

Before you can start looking for job opportunities, it's important to take a step back and understand your strengths and abilities. This self-awareness can help you identify what you bring to the table and what kind of work you would enjoy and excel in.

One way to do this is to make a list of your past experiences, both in the workplace and outside of it. This can include volunteer work, hobbies, and other activities that showcase your skills and strengths. Another option is to take a personality test or skills assessment to gain a more in-depth understanding of your abilities and interests.

Here's an exercise to help you understand your strengths and abilities:

Make a list of your past experiences: Write down every experience you've had that showcases your skills and strengths. This can include volunteer work, hobbies, and other activities.

Reflect on each experience: Take a moment to think about what you learned from each experience, what you enjoyed about it, and what skills you developed.

Identify patterns: Look for patterns in the experiences you've listed. Are there certain tasks or activities that you seem to enjoy more than others? Do you have a particular skill that you seem to excel in?

Take a personality test or skills assessment: There are many online tests that can help you gain a better understanding of your personality, strengths, and abilities. These tests can provide valuable insights into what kind of work you would enjoy and excel in.

Seek feedback from others: Ask friends, family members, or colleagues for their opinions on your strengths and abilities. This feedback can provide valuable insights and help you see yourself in a different light.

B. Identifying Job Opportunities That Align with Your Skills and Interests

Once you have a better understanding of your skills and interests, you can start to identify job opportunities that align with them. You can do this by researching different industries and job types, as well as networking with friends, family, and professional contacts.

It's important to keep an open mind and not limit yourself to a specific industry or job type. You may find that a career you never considered before is a good fit for your skills and interests.

In conclusion, taking the time to assess your skills and interests can help you make informed decisions about your career path and job search. Remember, it's never too late to start exploring new opportunities and finding a job that brings you fulfillment and stability.

III: Creating a Job Search Plan

In the wake of abuse or stalking, creating a stable source of income can be a crucial step towards rebuilding your life. One of the key components of this process is creating a job search plan. This involves setting goals and objectives, developing a strategy, and networking with potential employers. Here are some tips to help you create a successful job search plan.

A. Setting Goals and Objectives for Your Job Search

Setting clear goals and objectives for your job search can help you stay focused and motivated as you navigate this process. Start by considering what you want to achieve, both in the short-term and the long-term. This may include finding a job that provides a certain level of income, working in a specific industry, or pursuing a certain career path. Once you have a clear idea of your goals, you can use this information to guide your job search and make informed decisions about the opportunities that you pursue.

pursue. Place these items on a poster board or bulletin board where you can see them every day. This will help you stay focused and motivated as you work towards your goals.

Another exercise is to write down your goals in detail. Be as specific as possible, including the type of job, industry, salary, and location you are looking for. Review this list regularly and update it as you make progress in your job search. Use this list to guide your decisions and prioritize your job search activities.

Finally, consider reaching out to a mentor or career coach to help you set and achieve your job search goals. They can provide guidance, advice, and support as you work towards finding the right job for you.

B. Developing a Strategy for Finding Job Opportunities

Once you have set your goals and objectives, it's time to develop a strategy for finding job opportunities. This may involve leveraging your existing network, reaching out to recruiters and headhunters, or using job search websites and databases. It's important to be proactive and persistent in your search, and to take advantage of every opportunity that comes your way. Remember, finding a job is a full-time job in itself, and it requires a strong commitment and a lot of hard work.

Networking: Make a list of everyone you know who works in the industry or field you are interested in. Reach out to them and ask if they know of any job opportunities or if they would be willing to introduce you to someone in their network. Attend industry events, conferences, and meetups to expand your network and connect with potential employers.

Job Search Websites and Databases: Use job search websites and databases, such as Indeed, LinkedIn, and Glassdoor, to find job postings and research potential employers. Set up job alerts to receive notifications of new postings that match your skills and interests.

Practice: Consider conducting mock interviews and preparing answers to common interview questions to help you feel more confident and prepared during real interviews.

Consistency: Make job searching a part of your daily routine and persist in your efforts, even when you face rejection. Remember, it may take time to find the right opportunity, but staying focused and persistent will pay off in the end.

C. Networking and Building Connections with Potential Employers

Networking is a critical component of any job search, and it can be especially important if you are looking to build a stable source of income after abuse or stalking. By building relationships with potential employers and other professionals in your field, you can gain insights into job opportunities, learn about the latest industry trends, and gain a competitive edge over other job seekers. Whether you attend industry events, join professional organizations, or simply connect with people in your network, be sure to take advantage of every opportunity to build meaningful connections and grow your network.

In conclusion, creating a job search plan is a critical step towards finding a stable source of income after abuse or stalking. By setting clear goals, developing a strategy, and networking with potential employers, you can increase your chances of success and build the foundation for a better future.

IV: Applying for Jobs and Preparing for Interviews

As you continue on your journey towards financial stability, it's time to start applying for jobs and preparing for interviews. This can be a nerve-wracking experience, but with the right preparation and mindset, you can feel confident and ready to take on the challenge.

your skills and experiences, while also highlighting what makes you unique.

When writing your resume, focus on your accomplishments and how they relate to the job you're applying for. Your cover letter should also be tailored to each job you apply for and should highlight your passion for the work and why you believe you would be a good fit for the company.

Here's a template for writing a strong resume and cover letter:

Resume:

I. Introduction:

Brief summary of your experience and qualifications (1-2 sentences)
II. Work Experience:

List of your past work experiences, starting with the most recent
Include the company name, your job title, dates of employment, and key responsibilities and achievements
Use bullet points to make your experience easy to read
III. Education:

List of your degrees and certifications, starting with the highest level of education
Include the name of the institution, the degree you received, and the dates you attended
IV. Skills:

List of your key skills, including technical skills and soft skills
Consider highlighting skills that are relevant to the job you're applying for
V. Awards and Accomplishments:

List of any awards or recognition you've received for your work

Reiterate your interest in the position and why you believe you would be a good fit

Thank the reader for their time and consideration

Cover Letter:

I. Introduction:

Address the letter to a specific person (if possible)

Mention the position you're applying for and how you found out about the opportunity

Explain why you're interested in the position and what makes you a good fit

II. Body:

Provide specific examples of your experience and achievements that are relevant to the position you're applying for

Highlight how your skills and experiences align with the requirements of the job

Explain why you're interested in working for the company and what you can bring to the table

III. Conclusion:

Reiterate your interest in the position and your qualifications for the role

Ask for an opportunity to further discuss your application

Provide your contact information and thank the reader for their time

This template provides a basic framework for creating a strong resume and cover letter. It's important to tailor your resume and cover letter to the specific job you're applying for, and to highlight your most relevant skills and experiences.

do your research on the company. This can help you better understand their culture and mission, as well as give you a better understanding of what the job entails.

It's also important to prepare for the interview by practicing common interview questions, researching the company's values and mission, and preparing a list of questions to ask the interviewer. This shows that you're knowledgeable, interested, and invested in the job.

C. Tips for Making a Positive Impression During an Interview

When it comes to the interview itself, it's important to be confident and approach the experience with a positive attitude. Here are a few tips to help you make a good impression:

➢ Dress appropriately and arrive on time
➢ Show enthusiasm and interest in the job
➢ Be yourself and let your personality shine through
➢ Highlight your strengths and experiences, and how they relate to the job
➢ Be prepared to ask thoughtful questions and show interest in the company and its goals.

Remember, the interview is your opportunity to make a strong impression and to showcase why you would be the right fit for the job. By approaching the experience with confidence and positivity, you can increase your chances of success and take another step towards creating a stable source of income.

V: Building a Stable Source of Income

Introduction:

In the aftermath of abuse or stalking, it's important to focus on rebuilding your life and creating a stable foundation for your future. One of the key components of this foundation is a stable source of income. This means having a consistent flow of money that allows you

As survivors of abuse or stalking, we often face unique financial challenges and instability. Our attackers may have stolen our identity, damaged our credit, or left us with unexpected expenses. Additionally, the trauma of the experience can make it difficult to focus on work or hold down a job. That's why it's so important to build a stable source of income, as a way of regaining control over our lives and our finances.

II. Tips for Budgeting and Saving Money

A key component of creating a stable source of income is budgeting and saving money. This may involve reducing expenses, tracking your spending, and prioritizing your needs. You may also want to consider creating a budget that allows for some fun and relaxation, as this can help reduce stress and improve overall well-being. Additionally, it's important to create a savings plan that you can stick to, so that you have a cushion for unexpected expenses or emergencies.

III. Exploring Opportunities for Additional Income Streams

In addition to a regular job, there are many other ways to build a stable source of income. This may include freelancing, starting a side business, or finding ways to monetize your skills and interests. It's important to be creative and proactive as you explore these opportunities, and to be open to new ideas and possibilities. The goal is to build a source of income that is consistent, reliable, and flexible, so that you can have financial security and peace of mind.

Conclusion:

Building a stable source of income after abuse or stalking is an important step on the road to recovery. It's a way of regaining control over your life and your finances, and of creating a foundation for your future. Whether it's through a regular job, freelancing, or starting a side business, the key is to be proactive, persistent, and focused on your goals. With the right strategy and mindset, you can build a stable

As we come to the end of this chapter, I want to take a moment to reflect on what we've learned and emphasize the importance of perseverance and persistence in finding a job and building a stable source of income. Rebuilding your life after abuse or stalking can be a challenging and overwhelming process, but it's also a journey filled with opportunities for growth and transformation.

A. Summary of Key Takeaways

Throughout this chapter, we've discussed the importance of financial stability after abuse or stalking, and we've explored the various steps involved in finding a job and creating a consistent source of income. We've talked about assessing your skills and interests, creating a job search plan, preparing for interviews, and building a stable source of income.

B. Emphasizing the Importance of Perseverance and Persistence

As you embark on this journey, it's important to remember that finding a job and building a stable source of income requires perseverance and persistence. You may face setbacks and obstacles along the way, but it's important to keep moving forward and to never give up on your goals.

It's also important to be kind and gentle with yourself as you navigate this process. Rebuilding your life after abuse or stalking can be a long and emotional journey, and it's okay to take your time and to prioritize your well-being.

So, as you continue on this journey, I encourage you to be patient, persistent, and to never lose sight of your goals. With hard work, determination, and a commitment to your future, you can rebuild your life and create a stable and fulfilling future.

I. Introduction to Building Self-Esteem and a Positive Self-Image
A. Explanation of the impact of abuse or stalking on self-esteem and self-image
B. Overview of the importance of rebuilding self-esteem and creating a positive self-image

II. Understanding Your Thoughts and Beliefs About Yourself
A. Recognizing negative self-talk and challenging limiting beliefs
B. Examining the sources of your beliefs about yourself
C. Practicing self-compassion and treating yourself with kindness and respect

III. Building Confidence and Self-Worth
A. Engaging in activities that build confidence and self-esteem
B. Celebrating your accomplishments and successes
C. Fostering a growth mindset and embracing challenges as opportunities for growth

IV. Improving Physical Health and Appearance
A. Understanding the connection between physical health and self-esteem
B. Making healthy choices and engaging in physical activity
C. Taking care of personal grooming and dressing in a way that feels good to you

V. Connecting with Others and Building a Support System
A. Seeking support from family and friends
B. Joining support groups or therapy groups
C. Building new relationships and social connections

VI. Making Changes and Moving Forward
A. Taking action towards your goals and aspirations
B. Embracing change and new experiences
C. Letting go of the past and focusing on the present and future

C. Encouraging self-reflection and self-care to maintain and grow self-esteem and self-worth.

Dear friend,

I hope this message finds you well. My name is Melisa, and I am a survivor of abuse and stalking. I understand all too well the impact that these experiences can have on one's self-esteem and self-image. The words and actions of the abuser can leave you feeling shattered, powerless, and questioning your worth. However, I am here to tell you that you are strong, you are resilient, and you have the power to rebuild.

As someone who has been through the trauma of abuse or stalking, I want you to know that you are not alone. There are many of us who have gone through similar experiences, and we are all on our own journeys of healing and self-discovery. Throughout my own journey, I have learned the importance of prioritizing my own self-care and working to rebuild my self-esteem and self-image. It has been a challenging journey, but it has also been incredibly rewarding.

In this letter, I would like to share with you some of the strategies and tools I have used to regain my sense of self-worth and build a positive self-image. I hope that these lessons will inspire you to take the first steps in your own journey of self-discovery and self-empowerment.

A. Explanation of the Impact of Abuse or Stalking on Self-Esteem and Self-Image

The trauma of abuse or stalking can have a profound impact on your self-esteem and self-image. The words and actions of the abuser can leave you feeling like you are not good enough, and it can be difficult to shake these feelings. This is especially true if the abuse has been ongoing or has been at the hands of someone you loved and trusted.

take control of your life and rebuild your self-esteem and self-image. By doing so, you can regain a sense of self-worth and confidence, and you can start to see yourself as the strong and capable person that you truly are.

C. Strategies and Tools for Rebuilding Self-Esteem and Creating a Positive Self-Image

So, how can you start to rebuild your self-esteem and self-image? Here are some of the strategies and tools that have worked for me:

Seek out support from friends, family, or a professional counselor. Talking about your experiences and getting support from others can be incredibly healing.

Practice self-care. This can include taking care of your physical health, getting enough sleep, and engaging in activities that bring you joy and relaxation.

Surround yourself with positive people who support and encourage you. Avoid those who bring you down or make you feel worse about yourself.

Write down your strengths and accomplishments. This can help you focus on your positive qualities and begin to see yourself in a more positive light.

Challenge negative self-talk. When you find yourself thinking negative thoughts about yourself, stop and challenge those thoughts with positive self-affirmations.

Practice gratitude. Focusing on the things in your life that you are grateful for can help shift your focus away from the abuse or stalking and towards the positive.

Engage in activities that boost self-confidence. This can include learning a new skill, taking up a new hobby, or volunteering.

Introduction:

Surviving abuse or stalking can take a significant toll on your self-esteem and self-worth. It's normal to feel unsure of yourself, to doubt your abilities and to question your worth as a person. However, it's also important to understand that this is not a permanent state and that you have the power to change it. Through intentional effort, self-reflection and self-care, you can build a positive self-image and reclaim your self-esteem.

I know this because I've been there. I was a victim of abuse and it took me a long time to pick myself up and find my way back to feeling like myself again. But I did it, and so can you. This chapter will provide you with practical tips and exercises for building self-esteem and a positive self-image, so that you can feel confident and strong, no matter what challenges you face.

A. Explanation of the impact of abuse or stalking on self-esteem and self-image:

Abuse and stalking can have a devastating impact on a person's self-esteem and self-image. The constant barrage of negative comments, criticism, and insults can leave deep emotional scars and make it difficult to feel good about oneself. It's not uncommon for survivors to experience feelings of worthlessness, shame, and self-doubt as a result of their experiences.

In addition to the psychological effects, abuse and stalking can also have physical consequences that can impact one's self-image. For example, physical injuries and scars can serve as a constant reminder of the abuse, making it difficult to feel good about one's appearance.

creating a positive self-image, it is a critical step in the healing process. Having a healthy sense of self-worth and confidence can help survivors to move beyond the trauma of their experiences and reclaim their lives.

Whether it's through therapy, support groups, or simply engaging in activities that bring joy and fulfillment, there are many ways to begin the process of rebuilding self-esteem and creating a positive self-image. The most important thing is to be patient and kind to oneself, and to recognize that this is a journey that takes time and effort.

So if you're a survivor of abuse or stalking, know that you are not alone and that there is hope for a brighter future. By taking small steps and being intentional about your self-care, you can reclaim your sense of self-worth and build a positive self-image.

II. Understanding Your Thoughts and Beliefs About Yourself

Hello my friends,

I hope this chapter finds you well. I understand how difficult it can be to navigate the impact of abuse or stalking on one's self-esteem and self-image. However, I am here to tell you that there is hope, and you have the power to heal and rebuild. One of the most important steps in this process is understanding your thoughts and beliefs about yourself.

A. Recognizing negative self-talk and challenging limiting beliefs

The words we tell ourselves and the thoughts we have about ourselves can have a profound impact on our self-esteem and self-image. Negative self-talk, such as "I'm not good enough," "I don't deserve happiness," or "I'm weak," can be especially damaging. It's important to recognize when these thoughts arise and to challenge them. Ask yourself if these beliefs are really true, and try to replace them with positive affirmations. For example, you might tell yourself, "I am strong and capable," "I am deserving of love and happiness," or "I have the power to heal and grow."

on our self-esteem and self-image. Negative self-talk, such as "I'm not good enough," "I don't deserve happiness," or "I'm weak," can be especially damaging. These negative thoughts can feel like a vicious cycle, always bringing us down and making it difficult to feel good about ourselves.

Recognizing when these negative thoughts arise is the first step to breaking the cycle. Take a moment to listen to the thoughts that are running through your mind. Do you find yourself frequently criticizing yourself or putting yourself down? If so, it's time to start challenging these beliefs.

Challenging limiting beliefs requires questioning their validity. Ask yourself if these beliefs are really true. Can you think of evidence that contradicts these thoughts? It's important to remember that just because a thought pops into your mind doesn't mean it's accurate or true.

Once you've challenged these negative beliefs, it's time to replace them with positive affirmations. For example, you might tell yourself, "I am strong and capable," "I am deserving of love and happiness," or "I have the power to heal and grow." These positive affirmations can help you counteract the negative self-talk and start to build a more positive self-image.

Journal Exercises:

Keep a thought journal: Every day, write down the negative self-talk that you experience. Take note of the frequency of these thoughts and the specific things you tell yourself.

_____

_____

_____

_____

_____

_____

_____

_____

_____

_____

Identify the source of your negative beliefs: Ask yourself where these beliefs came from. Did you hear them from someone else, or did you come up with them yourself? Write down your answers in your thought journal.

_____

_____

_____

_____

_____

Replace negative self-talk with positive affirmations: Once you've identified the negative self-talk, write down a positive affirmation that counteracts it. Repeat these affirmations to yourself every day, and consider writing them down in a place where you can see them frequently.

_____

_____

_____

_____

_____

Practice self-compassion: Treat yourself with kindness and respect. When you catch yourself engaging in negative self-talk, remind

_____

_____

_____

_____

Reflect on your progress: At the end of each week, take some time to reflect on your progress. What positive affirmations have you been repeating to yourself? Have you noticed a decrease in negative self-talk? Write down your answers in your thought journal.

_____

_____

_____

_____

_____

Celebrate your successes: Every time you successfully challenge a negative belief or replace negative self-talk with a positive affirmation, take some time to celebrate your success. Write down what you did and how it made you feel in your thought journal.

B: Examining the Sources of Your Beliefs About Yourself

We all have beliefs about ourselves that shape our self-esteem and self-image. Some of these beliefs are positive and empowering, while others can be limiting and damaging. In order to build a positive self-image and increase our self-esteem, it's important to examine the sources of these beliefs.

Where do our beliefs about ourselves come from?

- ✧ The experiences and beliefs of those close to us
- ✧ Cultural and societal norms
- ✧ Childhood experiences and messages from parents, teachers, and other authority figures
- ✧ Trauma and abuse
- ✧ Why is it important to examine the sources of our beliefs?

Examining the sources of our beliefs can help us better understand why we have them. It can also help us challenge and change limiting beliefs that are holding us back. For example, if we have a belief that we're not good enough, we can examine where this belief came from. Did we hear this message from someone in our lives? Was it a result of our experiences or the experiences of those close to us? Understanding the origin of these beliefs can help us work to challenge and change them.

Journal exercises to examine the sources of your beliefs:

Write down your beliefs about yourself. Make a list of the beliefs that you have about yourself, both positive and negative.

_____

_____

_____

_____

Trace the origin of your beliefs. For each belief on your list, try to trace where it came from. Was it based on your experiences or the experiences of those close to you? Did you learn it from someone else? Was it a result of cultural or societal norms?

_____

_____

_____

Evaluate the validity of your beliefs. Take a closer look at each belief on your list. Are these beliefs really true? Can you think of evidence that contradicts these thoughts?

_____

_____

_____

_____

_____

Identify the impact of your beliefs on your life. How have these beliefs affected your self-esteem and self-image? Have they held you back in any way?

_____

_____

_____

_____

_____

Work to challenge and change limiting beliefs. Identify the beliefs that are holding you back and work to challenge and change them. Replace them with positive affirmations and start to build a more positive self-image.

_____

_____

_____

_____

_____

By examining the sources of your beliefs about yourself, you can gain a deeper understanding of why you have them and work to

As a survivor of abuse or stalking, you have been through a great deal of trauma and difficulty. It's important to be gentle with yourself and practice self-compassion. Treating yourself with kindness and respect is a critical part of your journey to healing and self-discovery.

One of the most important things you can do for yourself is to engage in self-care. This might mean taking a relaxing bath, going for a walk, or indulging in your favorite hobby. By taking care of yourself, you are sending a message to yourself that you deserve love and happiness.

Another important aspect of self-compassion is speaking to yourself in a kind and gentle manner. Imagine if a friend was going through what you're going through. How would you speak to them? Would you criticize them and put them down? Of course not! You would be there for them with love and support. Try to speak to yourself in the same way.

It's also important to remember that you deserve love and happiness. You have the power to create it for yourself. Surround yourself with positive and supportive people, and engage in activities that bring you joy and happiness. This might mean volunteering, spending time with friends, or exploring new hobbies.

Practicing self-compassion and treating yourself with kindness and respect is an ongoing process. It takes time and effort, but the rewards are well worth it. By being gentle with yourself and creating a positive and loving environment, you are giving yourself the space to heal, grow, and discover your true self.

Journal Exercises:

Write down three things you did for yourself today that were acts of self-care.

Write down three kind and loving things you would say to a friend who was going through a difficult time. Now, write down three kind and loving things you can say to yourself.

_____

_____

_____

_____

_____

Write down one way you can show yourself love and kindness this week.

_____

_____

_____

_____

_____

Write a letter to yourself, expressing self-compassion and love.

Remember, you deserve love and happiness. Be gentle with yourself, and allow yourself the space to heal and grow.

Example:

Dear [Your Name],

I hope this letter finds you in good health and spirits. Today, I want to take a moment to write to you about self-compassion and love. I want to remind you that you are deserving of love and kindness, especially from yourself.

simply part of the human experience.

I want you to be gentle with yourself. Talk to yourself with kindness and understanding, just as you would to a dear friend. Acknowledge your emotions, whether they be positive or negative, and allow yourself to feel them without judgment.

Take care of yourself, both physically and mentally. Nourish your body with healthy food, exercise regularly, and get enough sleep. Engage in activities that bring you joy and relaxation. Seek help if you are struggling with negative thoughts or emotions.

I want you to know that you are worthy of love and happiness, and that you deserve to live a fulfilling life. You are capable of achieving your dreams and reaching your goals, but that starts with loving and accepting yourself exactly as you are.

Remember to be kind and compassionate to yourself, always.

With love,

[Your Name]

I hope these tips will help you as you begin to understand your thoughts and beliefs about yourself. Remember, healing and growth take time, but they are possible. Keep persevering and be kind to yourself.

Wishing you all the best,

- Melisa

PART VII.
MOVING FORWARD

II. Understanding the Stages of Grief and Recovery
A. Denial
B. Anger
C. Bargaining
D. Depression
E. Acceptance
F. Navigating the Journey of Recovery

III. Facing Your Fears and Taking Control of Your Life
A. Identifying Your Fears
B. Developing a Plan to Overcome Your Fears
C. Embracing Change and Moving Forward

IV. Finding Your Purpose and Building a Fulfilling Life
A. Discovering Your Passions and Interests
B. Setting Goals and Creating a Vision for Your Life
C. Building a Support System

V. Conclusion: Embracing Your Journey of Healing and Moving Forward
A. Reflecting on Your Progress
B. Celebrating Your Accomplishments
C. Moving Forward with Hope and Resilience.

As a survivor, I understand the challenges and complexities of moving forward after trauma. It's not an easy process, but it's one that is necessary for growth and healing. The journey may be long and difficult, but the reward at the end is a life filled with purpose and joy.

Brené Brown, a renowned researcher and storyteller, has dedicated her life's work to exploring the topics of vulnerability, courage, and shame. Through her research, she has found that moving forward and embracing our vulnerability is essential to building a fulfilling life.

Together, we will explore the stages of grief and recovery, facing our fears, and finding our purpose. We will also share tips and strategies to help you on your journey towards a happier, more fulfilling life. Remember, you are not alone, and it's okay to ask for help and support along the way.

With love and support,

Melisa

I. Introduction to Moving Forward
A. The Importance of Moving Forward

Dear reader,

Welcome to the journey of moving forward. As a survivor, I understand the challenges of healing and recovery and the importance of taking steps to move forward in life. Whether you are recovering from a traumatic experience, overcoming addiction, or working through a difficult time, the journey to healing and recovery can be a long and challenging one. But it is also a journey that is filled with hope, growth, and the potential for a brighter future.

resilience to overcome the challenges ahead.

One of the biggest challenges in healing and recovery is overcoming feelings of shame, guilt, or self-blame. It is important to recognize that these feelings are not your fault and that you are not to blame for what has happened to you. Instead, focus on self-compassion and self-care, and surround yourself with supportive friends and family members who can provide comfort and encouragement.

Another challenge in the healing and recovery process is facing the trauma head-on and confronting difficult emotions and memories. This can be difficult and overwhelming, but it is necessary in order to fully heal and move forward. Seek support from a therapist or support group, and take the time to process your emotions in a healthy way.

Finally, it is important to recognize that healing and recovery is a journey, not a destination. There will be ups and downs, and setbacks are to be expected. But with perseverance, determination, and self-care, you will find the strength to overcome these challenges and move forward towards a brighter future.

In conclusion, moving forward is a journey that is filled with hope, growth, and the potential for a brighter future. As a survivor, you have the strength and resilience to overcome the challenges of healing and recovery and to move forward in a positive direction.

III. Understanding the Stages of Grief and Recovery

A. Denial

Dear reader,

As a researcher and writer on topics such as vulnerability, shame, and empathy, I have had the opportunity to explore the complexities of the human experience, including the stages of grief and recovery.

defense mechanism that helps us to cope with the overwhelming emotions that we are feeling.

B. Anger: A Vital Part of the Healing Journey

As a researcher and storyteller, I have come to understand that anger is an inevitable part of the grieving process. It is a natural response to loss, trauma, and injustice. When we feel angry, it is because we are hurting, and we need to validate those feelings in order to heal.

When we are in the anger stage, it is not uncommon to feel overwhelmed by emotions. We may lash out at others, blame them for our situation, or feel that the world is against us. However, it is important to remember that anger is not just a negative emotion; it is also a powerful motivator. By channeling our anger in a constructive way, we can use it to drive us forward and to help us find the strength to heal.

One of the biggest challenges of the anger stage is that we may feel stuck. We may feel like we are not making any progress, or that we are trapped in a cycle of frustration and resentment. But this is simply not true. With time, patience, and self-reflection, we can work through our anger and begin to understand what is causing it.

One of the best ways to do this is through therapy or counseling. Talking to a trained professional can help us to understand the root of our anger and to find ways to manage it. We may also find comfort in support groups or in talking to others who have been through similar experiences.

Another important aspect of the anger stage is self-care. This can include things like exercise, mindfulness, and creative expression. By taking care of ourselves, we can begin to feel more in control of our emotions and more equipped to deal with the challenges of healing and recovery.

C. Bargaining: Seeking Meaning in the Face of Loss

Bargaining is a critical stage in the journey of grief and recovery. It is during this stage that we often try to make sense of the loss and trauma that we have experienced. We may find ourselves seeking answers, making deals with a higher power, or looking for a way to find meaning in the midst of our pain.

For many of us, bargaining is a way of trying to regain control. We may feel like life has dealt us an unfair blow, and that we are powerless to change our situation. However, by bargaining, we are essentially saying that we are willing to do anything to make things better. We are expressing our hope that there is a way to fix what has been broken.

It is important to remember that bargaining is a normal and natural part of the grieving process. It is a way for us to begin to come to terms with our loss and to begin to see a path forward. While it can be tempting to try and find a quick fix, or to make a deal with the universe to make everything okay, it is important to be patient and to allow ourselves the time and space to work through our feelings.

One of the best ways to do this is through therapy or counseling. Talking to a trained professional can help us to understand the root of our bargaining and to find ways to process it in a healthy and supportive way. We may also find comfort in support groups or in talking to others who have been through similar experiences.

It is also important to practice self-care during the bargaining stage. This can include things like exercise, mindfulness, and creative expression. By taking care of ourselves, we can begin to feel more in control of our emotions and more equipped to deal with the challenges of healing and recovery.

D. Depression

The fourth stage of grief and recovery is a crucial part of the journey. In this stage, we may find ourselves grappling with feelings of sadness, loneliness, and despair. It is natural to feel overwhelmed in the aftermath of a traumatic experience, and to question the meaning and purpose of life. This stage is often referred to as depression, and it is important to understand that it is a normal part of the healing process.

At this stage, it is important to allow yourself to feel the emotions that are arising, without judgment or criticism. Depression can be a heavy and isolating experience, but it is important to remember that you are not alone. Many people have gone through similar experiences and have come out the other side.

It is important to find support during this stage, whether that be from friends, family, a therapist, or a support group. Talking to someone who can understand and support you can help to alleviate some of the feelings of loneliness and isolation. You may also find it helpful to engage in activities that bring you joy and comfort, such as hobbies, exercise, or spending time with loved ones.

It is also important to take care of your physical health during this stage. Making sure to eat well, get enough sleep, and engage in physical activity can help to improve your mood and overall well-being.

It is important to remember that depression is not permanent. While it can be a difficult stage, it will eventually pass, and you will begin to see glimpses of hope and positivity once again. Trust in the journey of healing and recovery, and know that you are not alone. With time, patience, and self-care, you will begin to move beyond this stage and towards acceptance and growth.

bargaining, and depression, we finally reach a place of acceptance. This stage is not necessarily about forgetting what happened or forgiving those who may have caused harm, but it's about acknowledging the reality of the situation and finding a way to move forward.

At this stage, survivors may still experience feelings of pain and sadness, but they also start to feel a sense of hope and a new direction in life. It's important to understand that acceptance is not a one-time event, but rather a gradual process. It may take time and patience, but it's a crucial step in the healing journey.

In this stage, it's important to continue to be gentle with yourself and to focus on self-care and self-compassion. Surround yourself with supportive friends and family, and seek help from a mental health professional if needed. Try to focus on finding a new purpose or meaning in life, whether it's through work, hobbies, volunteering, or spending time with loved ones.

For many survivors, acceptance can also involve letting go of the past and forgiving oneself for any perceived mistakes or shortcomings. It's important to remember that you did the best you could in the situation and that it's not your fault.

By embracing acceptance, survivors can finally start to find peace and hope for the future. They can begin to rebuild their lives and find joy and happiness once again. Remember, healing is a journey and it takes time, but by focusing on self-care and compassion, you can finally reach a place of acceptance and find a new sense of hope and purpose in life.

F. Navigating the Journey of Recovery

As a survivor, it is normal to feel overwhelmed, lost, and unsure of what to do next as you navigate the journey of recovery. The road ahead may seem long and uncertain, but it is important to remember that you are not alone. You have the strength and resilience within you friends, family members, or a mental health professional. Talking about your feelings and experiences with someone who cares about you can help you to process your thoughts and emotions, and to feel less isolated and alone.

It's also important to take care of yourself as you navigate this journey. This might include engaging in self-care activities, such as exercising, meditating, or practicing mindfulness. Taking time to rest and recharge can help you to feel more energized, focused, and ready to face the challenges ahead.

It's also important to be patient with yourself and to recognize that the journey of recovery is a process, not a destination. There will be good days and bad days, and that's okay. Remember that healing is not linear, and that it is normal to experience setbacks and setbacks along the way. It's also important to have compassion for yourself and to acknowledge your own feelings and experiences, rather than trying to suppress or ignore them.

Finally, it's important to have a sense of purpose and meaning as you navigate this journey. This might involve finding new hobbies or interests, volunteering, or pursuing a career that aligns with your values and passions. By focusing on what gives your life meaning and purpose, you can channel your energy and enthusiasm into something that brings you joy and fulfillment.

In conclusion, navigating the journey of grief and recovery can be challenging, but it is also an opportunity for growth, healing, and transformation. By seeking support, taking care of yourself, being patient with yourself, and having a sense of purpose, you can find the peace and hope that you are searching for.

IV. Conclusion

In conclusion, as a survivor, I want to remind you that the journey of healing and recovery is not a linear process. It is filled with ups and

I have learned that understanding the stages of grief and recovery can be incredibly helpful in navigating the journey of healing. By recognizing where you are in the process, you can better understand what you need and what steps you can take to move forward. Whether that means seeking support from friends, family, or mental health professionals, or engaging in self-care and self-compassion, the important thing is to be kind and patient with yourself as you navigate this journey.

In the end, I want to remind you that you are more than your experiences, and that you have the power to create a new future for yourself. You have survived this far, and you will continue to do so. You will find hope and happiness again, and you will come out of this journey stronger, more resilient, and more capable of facing whatever life may bring your way.

Here are some journal exercises that can help you work through each of the stages of grief and recovery:

A. Anger:

Write down all the things that are causing you to feel angry right now. Try to be specific and name the people, events, or situations that are contributing to your anger.

_____

_____

_____

_____

_____

Reflect on why you're feeling angry. What are the underlying emotions and beliefs that are fueling your anger?

_____

Write a letter to the person, event, or situation that is causing your anger. In this letter, express your feelings and thoughts without any filters or censorship. You don't have to send the letter, but it can be cathartic to write it out.

Template:

Dear [Person, Event, or Situation],

I hope this letter finds you well. I am writing to express my feelings and thoughts about what has been causing me anger.

I am feeling [insert emotions], and I want you to know that [insert reasons for feeling this way]. I feel [insert additional emotions] because [insert reasons for these emotions].

[Optional: Insert any specific incidents or events that have contributed to your anger].

I understand that [insert reasons for the person, event, or situation causing your anger], but it still affects me in a negative way. I want you to know that I am doing my best to cope with these feelings, but it is not easy.

[Optional: Insert any requests or demands you may have in regards to the situation].

I just wanted to let you know how I am feeling and what has been going on inside of me. I hope that this letter helps to provide some clarity and understanding.

Sincerely,
[Your Name]

_____

_____

_____

_____

_____

B. Denial:

Write down all the things you are feeling right now. Try to name your emotions and describe what you're feeling in detail.

_____

_____

_____

_____

_____

Reflect on why you might be feeling in denial about your situation. Are you afraid of facing the reality of what has happened? Are you trying to protect yourself from feeling pain?

_____

_____

_____

_____

_____

Write down three things that you can do to help you move towards accepting the reality of what has happened. This could include things like talking to a trusted friend, reaching out to a therapist, or reading a book on grief and recovery.

_____

_____

_____

Write down one thing you are looking forward to in the future. This could be something small like your next meal or something larger like a trip you have planned. Focusing on the future can help you move out of denial and into acceptance.

C. Bargaining:

Write down all the things you are feeling right now. Try to name your emotions and describe what you're feeling in detail.

_____

_____

_____

_____

_____

Reflect on why you might be feeling like you want to bargain or make a deal. Are you trying to avoid the reality of what has happened? Are you feeling like you can control the situation if you just find the right solution?

_____

_____

_____

_____

_____

Write down three things you can do to help you move towards accepting the reality of what has happened. This could include things like talking to a trusted friend, reaching out to a therapist, or reading a book on grief and recovery.

_____

_____

Write down one thing you are grateful for in your life right now. Gratitude can help shift your focus from bargaining to acceptance.

D. Seeking Meaning in the Face of Loss:

Write down what you have lost. Try to describe your loss in detail, including what it means to you and how it has impacted your life.

_____

_____

_____

_____

_____

Reflect on what you have gained through your loss. This might be difficult, but try to focus on the positive aspects of your situation, no matter how small they may be.

_____

_____

_____

_____

_____

Write down three things you want to do to honor your loss. This could include things like creating a memorial, volunteering, or writing a letter to your loved one.

_____

_____

_____

_____

_____

_____

_____

_____

_____

_____

E. Depression:

Write down all the things you are feeling right now. Try to name your emotions and describe what you're feeling in detail.

_____

_____

_____

_____

_____

Reflect on why you might be feeling depressed. Are you feeling overwhelmed by your loss or life situation? Are you feeling like there is no hope or meaning in your life right now?

_____

_____

_____

_____

_____

Write down three things you can do to help you move out of depression. This could include things such as engaging in self-care activities, reaching out to a support system, and setting small achievable goals. Practicing gratitude by writing down things you are thankful for, engaging in physical activity, and challenging negative thoughts with positive affirmations can also help alleviate symptoms of

PART 8
CONCLUSION

You've been through a storm, a battle that tested your strength and resilience. You've faced challenges, fought through pain, and emerged stronger than ever. Your journey has been a testament to the human spirit, a shining example of what it means to persevere. And now, as you reach the end of this journey, it's time to take a deep breath, look back, and celebrate your achievements.

You've traveled a road that many others before you have not been able to complete. You've conquered fears, overcome obstacles, and discovered a new sense of hope and purpose. And in doing so, you've shown the world what it truly means to be a survivor. You've proven that no matter what life throws your way, you have the strength, the courage, and the determination to rise above it.

In these final pages, we want to offer you words of encouragement, inspiration, and empowerment. We want to remind you that the journey is far from over, that there are new adventures ahead, and that your future is brighter than you can imagine. We want to inspire you to keep fighting, to keep dreaming, and to keep pushing forward. And we want to empower you to take control of your life, to make the changes you want to see, and to create the life you deserve.

So take a deep breath, dear survivors, and get ready to take that final step. Get ready to turn the page, to begin a new chapter, and to start a new journey. The future is yours, and it's time to seize it with both hands.

SURVIVORS

I. Introduction

Acknowledge the journey that survivors have been through and the challenges they have faced.
Highlight the importance of encouragement and empowerment in the recovery process.

II. The Power of Encouragement

Discuss the role that encouragement plays in helping survivors overcome obstacles and build resilience.
Share inspiring stories and examples of how encouragement has helped others in their recovery journeys.

III. Building Empowerment

Define empowerment and explain why it is crucial in the recovery process.
Outline practical steps for building and maintaining a sense of empowerment, such as setting achievable goals and developing positive self-talk.

IV. Overcoming Obstacles

Discuss common obstacles that survivors face on the road to recovery, such as negative self-talk and feelings of hopelessness.
Provide guidance on how to overcome these obstacles and maintain a positive outlook.

V. Conclusion

Summarize the importance of encouragement and empowerment for survivors.

obstacles along the way. This journey can be overwhelming, but it is also a journey of growth and transformation. As a survivor, you are a testament to the strength and resilience of the human spirit, and it is important to acknowledge and celebrate your journey.

The Importance of Encouragement and Empowerment

Encouragement and empowerment are essential components of the recovery process. When we are feeling down and defeated, encouragement and support can help us to pick ourselves up and keep going. When we are empowered, we feel confident and capable, and this can help us to overcome the obstacles in our path.

Encouragement and empowerment can come from many sources. It can come from friends and family, from mental health professionals, or from within. It is important to seek out support and encouragement from these sources and to take the time to celebrate your progress and your victories, no matter how small they may be.

A Message of Hope

As a survivor, you have faced many challenges, but you have also overcome many obstacles. You are a testament to the strength and resilience of the human spirit, and you are a source of inspiration and hope to others. You are a hero in your own right, and you should be proud of all that you have accomplished.

Conclusion

Encouragement and empowerment are essential components of the recovery process. They can help us to pick ourselves up and keep going, even when the road ahead seems long and difficult. As a survivor, you are a source of hope and inspiration, and you should celebrate your journey and the victories that you have achieved along the way. Remember, you are not alone, and you have the strength and resilience to overcome the challenges that lie ahead.

to overcome the obstacles that come with healing and recovery. But what if I told you that there is a powerful tool that can help you along the way? A tool that can boost your confidence, reduce your stress, and help you find hope for the future? That tool is encouragement.

Encouragement is a simple but powerful act of kindness that can have a profound impact on a person's life. When we receive encouragement, it helps us feel seen and heard, and it can give us the strength to keep going when we feel like giving up. Encouragement can come in many forms, including words of affirmation, gestures of support, or simple acts of kindness.

There are countless stories of survivors who have been empowered and inspired by encouragement from friends, family, and even strangers. Take for example, Sarah, who lost her home in a devastating fire. She felt overwhelmed and hopeless until a group of volunteers from a local church came to help her clean up the rubble. They encouraged her to keep going, to not give up hope, and reminded her that she was not alone in her journey. With their encouragement, Sarah found the strength to start over and rebuild her life.

Or consider Michael, who was struggling with depression after losing his job. He felt worthless and unimportant until a friend took the time to sit down and have a heart-to-heart conversation with him. The friend encouraged Michael to focus on his strengths and to look for new opportunities, reminding him that he was capable and worthy of success. With this encouragement, Michael was able to find a new job and get back on track with his life.

Encouragement can come from anyone and it doesn't have to be elaborate or grand. Sometimes, it can be as simple as a compliment, a smile, or a kind word. Encouragement can be a source of light in the darkness, a source of hope in the face of despair.

In conclusion, the power of encouragement should never be underestimated. Whether you are a survivor or a loved one, it is important to seek out encouragement and to offer encouragement to

Empowerment is the process of gaining control over your life and feeling capable of making positive changes. In the context of recovery, empowerment is about taking an active role in your healing journey and building resilience. It is about regaining a sense of control over your life after feeling vulnerable and powerless. Empowerment is crucial in the recovery process because it gives survivors the strength and confidence they need to overcome the challenges they face.

Here are some practical steps for building and maintaining a sense of empowerment:

Set achievable goals: Setting and working towards achievable goals can help you feel a sense of accomplishment and progress. These goals could be related to physical or mental health, personal growth, or anything else that you value.

Develop positive self-talk: Your thoughts have a powerful impact on your emotions and actions. Practice speaking to yourself with kindness and positivity, and replace negative thoughts with positive affirmations.

Practice self-care: Taking care of your physical, emotional, and mental well-being is an important part of building empowerment. This can include things like eating a nutritious diet, getting regular exercise, and engaging in activities that bring you joy and relaxation.

Surround yourself with supportive people: Building a strong support system can help you feel encouraged and empowered. Surround yourself with friends and family who uplift you and provide a safe space for you to express your thoughts and feelings.

Take action: Empowerment is about taking control of your life and making positive changes. Take action towards your goals, even if it means facing your fears.

purpose and fulfillment.

IV. Overcoming Obstacles

As survivors, we face many challenges on the road to recovery. At times, it may feel like the obstacles are too great to overcome and that we will never be able to move forward. But the truth is, with the right tools and support, we can overcome any obstacle that comes our way.

One of the biggest obstacles that survivors face is negative self-talk. When we experience loss or trauma, it can be easy to fall into a pattern of negative thoughts and beliefs about ourselves. We may feel like we are not strong enough, capable enough, or deserving enough of a bright future.

However, it is important to recognize that these negative thoughts are not true. They are simply a result of our experiences and a way for our minds to try and make sense of what has happened. To overcome this obstacle, we need to work on changing our negative self-talk into positive and empowering self-talk.

Another obstacle that survivors face is feelings of hopelessness. When we have been through so much, it can be hard to see a future that is filled with joy and happiness. But it is important to remember that there is always hope, no matter how small it may seem. We can find hope in the people who love us, in our passions and interests, and in the knowledge that we are capable of overcoming anything that comes our way.

To maintain a positive outlook and overcome these obstacles, it is important to seek support from friends, family, and mental health professionals. We should also engage in self-care activities that bring us joy and happiness, and work on building resilience and strength through exercise and mindfulness practices.

Remember, as survivors, we are stronger than we think. With determination, perseverance, and a little bit of hope, we can overcome challenges and overcome obstacles, and we have learned the importance of encouragement and empowerment in our recovery journeys. The road to recovery is not always easy, but with the right tools and support, we can continue to grow, heal, and thrive.

The power of encouragement cannot be overstated. When we receive encouragement from others, it gives us the strength and motivation to keep going. It reminds us that we are not alone, and that there are people who care about us and believe in us. Whether it's a supportive friend, a kind word from a stranger, or a simple smile, encouragement can have a profound impact on our lives.

Empowerment is also crucial in our recovery journeys. When we feel empowered, we have a sense of control over our lives and a greater sense of self-worth. We feel confident in our ability to make positive changes, and we are more likely to reach our goals and live fulfilling lives. To build empowerment, it's important to set achievable goals, develop positive self-talk, and surround ourselves with supportive people.

Obstacles will arise along the way, but with determination and a positive outlook, we can overcome them. Negative self-talk and feelings of hopelessness are common obstacles, but we can counteract these negative thoughts by focusing on our strengths, practicing gratitude, and reaching out for support when needed.

In conclusion, as survivors, we have the strength and resilience to overcome any obstacle and achieve our goals. The journey to recovery is not always easy, but with encouragement, empowerment, and the right support, we can find hope, happiness, and a brighter future. So, let us continue to seek help and support as needed, and let us encourage and empower each other along the way.